OUR LIVING CONSTITUTION

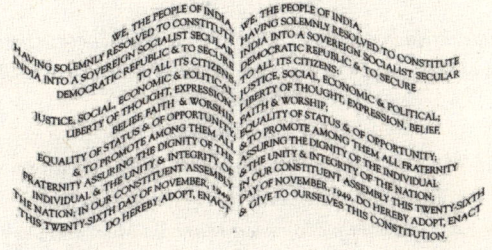

This title is the first of a series of books entitled
ESSENTIAL INDIA EDITIONS. Each book in the series will explore a
foundational aspect of the country in new and thought-provoking ways.
~

ALSO BY SHASHI THAROOR

NON-FICTION
A Wonderland of Words: Around the Word in 101 Essays
The Less You Preach the More You Learn: Aphorisms for Our Age
(with Joseph Zacharias)
Ambedkar: A Life
Pride, Prejudice, and Punditry: The Essential Shashi Tharoor
The Battle of Belonging: On Nationalism, Patriotism, and What It Means to Be Indian
Tharoorosaurus
The New World Disorder and the Indian Imperative (with Samir Saran)
The Hindu Way: An Introduction to Hinduism
The Paradoxical Prime Minister: Narendra Modi and His India
Why I Am a Hindu
An Era of Darkness: The British Empire in India
India Shastra: Reflections on the Nation in Our Time
India: The Future Is Now (ed.)
Pax Indica: India and the World of the 21st Century
Shadows Across the Playing Field: 60 Years of India-Pakistan Cricket (with Shahryar Khan)
India (with Ferrante Ferranti)
The Elephant, the Tiger, and the Cell Phone: Reflections on India in the 21st Century
Bookless in Baghdad
Nehru: The Invention of India
Kerala: God's Own Country (with M. F. Husain)
India: From Midnight to the Millennium and Beyond
Reasons of State

FICTION
Riot
Show Business
The Five Dollar Smile and Other Stories
The Great Indian Novel

OUR LIVING CONSTITUTION

A Concise Introduction & Commentary

SHASHI THAROOR

ALEPH BOOK COMPANY
An independent publishing firm
promoted by *Rupa Publications India*

First published in India in 2025
by Aleph Book Company
7/16 Ansari Road, Daryaganj
New Delhi 110 002

Copyright © Shashi Tharoor 2025

The author has asserted his moral rights.

All rights reserved.

Front cover illustration of the Ashoka Chakra: Wikimedia Commons; Parliament House illustration: Shutterstock/Snehit Photo

The views and opinions expressed in this book are those of the author and the facts are as reported by him, which have been verified to the extent possible, and the publisher is not in any way liable for the same.

The publisher has used its best endeavours to ensure that URLs for external websites referred to in this book are correct and active at the time of going to press. However, the publisher has no responsibility for the websites and can make no guarantee that a site will remain live or that the content is or will remain appropriate.

No part of this publication may be reproduced, transmitted, or stored in a retrieval system, in any form or by any means, without permission in writing from Aleph Book Company.

For sale in the Indian subcontinent only.

ISBN: 978-93-6523-372-8

5 7 9 10 8 6 4

Printed in India

This book is sold subject to the condition that it shall not, by way of trade or otherwise, be lent, resold, hired out, or otherwise circulated without the publisher's prior consent in any form of binding or cover other than that in which it is published.

In enduring memory
of
Dr Manmohan Singh
Who, over decades of service
To the people of India,
Breathed meaning into
The spirit of the Constitution,
This book is respectfully dedicated

Contents

Prologue ix

I   An Extraordinary Document   1

II   The Vision of the Founders   15

III   The Constitution and Indian Nationhood   25

IV   Elements of the Constitution   36

V   A Living Document   48

VI   Moving Beyond the Provisions   55

VII   An Alternative Idea of India   61

VIII   A Challenge to the Constitution Whither Secularism and Pluralism?   68

IX   A Union of States   85

Conclusion   96

Acknowledgements   107

Further Reading   109

Prologue

On 26 November 2024, Parliament held an unprecedented special session to celebrate the day seventy-five years earlier, on 26 November 1949, when the Constituent Assembly[1], the indirectly-elected 299-member body in charge of the task, finished its daunting task and agreed on a Constitution that was to be formally adopted two months later, on 26 January 1950.

That day, 26 November 1949, marked the conclusion of a long process of Constitution-making. The nationalist movement that gave our Constitution its legitimacy and sanctity had itself used many arguably non-constitutional methods in its struggle against imperial rule—non-cooperation, civil disobedience, satyagraha. Yet, it culminated in a democratic Constitution, the world's longest written Constitution for any nation and (or so many thought at the time) its most imperilled. Handwritten exquisitely in both English and Hindi by calligraphist Prem Behari Narain

---

[1] See, 'Constitution Making', Constitution of India. The Constituent Assembly first met on 9 December 1946. Members were elected by the Provincial Assemblies through a single transferable vote system of proportional representation. The Assembly initially had 389 members: 292 from British Indian provinces, 93 from princely states, and 4 from chief commissioner provinces. After the partition of India in 1947, the membership was reduced to 299. It held 11 sessions over a period of 2 years, 11 months, and 18 days, with the final session on 24 January 1950. The Constitution was adopted on 26 November 1949, and came into effect on 26 January 1950.

Raizada, each page adorned with intricate artwork inspired by Indian culture and heritage and designed by famous artists led by Nandalal Bose, the Constitution was not merely a legal document: it was a work of art. In its pages, to borrow Jawaharlal Nehru's famous metaphor, the soul of a nation, long suppressed, had found utterance.

On that occasion, Dr B. R. Ambedkar, chairman of the Drafting Committee of the Constituent Assembly, rose in what is now the Central Hall of the Samvidhan Sadan (the old Parliament House) to address his colleagues, his fellow Founding Fathers, with a prescient warning to the nation. 'However good a Constitution may be,' he said, 'it is sure to turn out bad because those who are called to work it, happen to be a bad lot. However bad a Constitution may be, it may turn out to be good if those who are called to work it, happen to be a good lot. The working of a Constitution does not depend wholly upon the nature of the Constitution.'[2]

It was a sobering reminder that the Constitution we celebrated then, as we celebrate it today, can be distorted and misused by 'wrong-minded' people in power.

As a staunch defender of democracy in both principle and practice, Dr Ambedkar anxiously wondered whether Indians would place 'the country above their creed'. He recalled the history of the Buddhist Bhikshu sanghas, which were known to have observed rules of modern-day parliamentary procedure, and added: 'This democratic system India lost. Will she lose it a second time? I do not know. But it is

---

[2] Abhijeet Pimparkar, 'The Grammar of Anarchy by Ambedkar', *Politics for India*, 8 July 2024; *Constituent Assembly Debates*, Vol. XI, 25 November 1949.

quite possible, in a country like India...there is danger of democracy giving place to dictatorship. It is quite possible for this newborn democracy to retain its form but give place to dictatorship in fact. If there is a landslide [victory], the danger of the second possibility becoming actuality is much greater.'[3]

His words haunt us today as we see a situation in which the affirmation of constitutional democracy through successive elections is followed by statements and actions unleashing intolerance and undemocratic values allowing them to run rampant in our society. Some might argue these have always occurred in a land as vast as India, but some recent trends are still disquieting. Political rhetoric by individuals unchallenged by the ruling party has demonized entire religious communities. Irresponsible statements of powerful members of the ruling party, including ministers, have served to divide our nation and our people, as communal polarization has been promoted for political reasons. The deaths of innocent people because of their faith, their professions, or even their alleged eating habits, have cast a shadow on our democracy. It is against this background that we examine our Constitution and how it has worked for the people of the world's largest democracy.

And yet, the Constitution is in vogue these days as never before. Scarcely does a ministerial speech fail to make a ritual genuflection to its all-pervasive majesty. Prime Minister Narendra Modi even used the occasion of his first address to the US Congress[4] in Washington in 2016 to inform

---

[3] Shashi Tharoor, 'Dont't Burn the Book of Freedom', *Open*, 16 June 2016.
[4] 'Full text of PM Modi's address to US Congress', *Times of India*, 9 June 2016.

the world that the Constitution was his only holy book. (Though it is the Bhagavad Gita, and not the Constitution, that he prefers to hand out on his visits to foreign leaders, the sentiment deserves appreciation.)

Jawaharlal Nehru had declared when moving the Objectives Resolution in the Constituent Assembly on 13 December 1946, as India embarked formally on the framing of a Constitution:

> It is a resolution and yet, it is something much more than a resolution. It is a declaration. It is a firm resolve. It is a pledge and an undertaking, and it is for all of us, I hope, a dedication. And I wish this house, if I may say so respectfully, should consider this resolution not in a spirit of narrow legal wording, but rather to look at the spirit behind that resolution.... [W]hen I think of the work of this Constituent Assembly, it seems to me the time is come when we should, as far as possible, rise above our ordinary selves and party disputes and think of the great problem before us in the widest and most tolerant and most effective manner, so that whatever we may produce, should be worthy of India as a whole and should be such that the world should recognize that we have functioned as we should have functioned in this high adventure.[5]

Why did the leaders choose 26 January for the Constitution to be officially adopted? Simply because of the fact that for the previous seventeen years, the Indian National Congress (INC) had celebrated 26 January as Independence Day. This commemorated the declaration of Independence issued by

---

[5] *Constituent Assembly Debates*, Vol. 1, 13 December 1946.

Jawaharlal Nehru, as president of the 1929 Lahore session of the INC, which called for 'Purna Swaraj' (total independence) to be established on 26 January 1930.[6] When Independence actually came on 15 August, the special associations of 26 January were preserved by making it our Republic Day, the day when the Constitution of India came into force.

'India's Constitution,' said Nelson Mandela, former president of South Africa and an unrivalled moral voice for freedom, is a 'beacon of hope' for the world, and 'provides inspiration in preparation of a new South African Constitution'. Mandela hoped that 'our efforts in formulation of a new constitution will reflect the work and ideas of this great son of India [Ambedkar].'[7] That high praise is typical of the way the Indian Constitution was hailed across the world. Its adoption was received almost rapturously by constitutional experts and scholars. Thomas R. Metcalf, the British historian, praised the Constitution for striking a balance between modern aspirations and traditional values: 'India's Constitution remains a rare and remarkable experiment of adapting Western liberal democracy to Indian conditions.'[8]

Other global eminences concurred. Indian leaders had set high standards of aspiration for themselves and felt they had achieved them. The president of the Constituent Assembly, who went on to serve as India's first president under the new Constitution, Dr Rajendra Prasad, declared that the Indian Constitution 'stands as a model for other nations,

---

[6] Asia Society: 'India's Republic Day: What You Need To Know'.
[7] 'Item 227 - Nelson Mandela's speech at the Indian Parliament on the unveiling of the statue of Pandit Jawaharlal Nehru and the commemoration of the founding of the Republic of India', Nelson Mandela Centre of Memory.
[8] Thomas R. Metcalf, *Forging the Raj: Essays on British India in the Heyday of Empire*, New Delhi: Oxford University Press, 2005.

demonstrating the importance of fundamental rights and freedoms.'[9] He added: 'The Constitution of India is not a mere legal document, it is a Magna Carta of the emancipation of the human spirit.'[10] As Ambedkar eloquently put it: 'Our Constitution provides us a magnificent structure beneath which all Indians, of all castes, creeds and languages, can equally seek shelter.'[11]

---

[9] *Constituent Assembly Debates*, Vol. 1, 11 December 1946.
[10] Quoted on the wall of the AICC Headquarters at Indira Bhavan, Kotla Marg, New Delhi.
[11] Vasant Moon (ed.), *Dr. Babasaheb Ambedkar: Writings and Speeches*, Vol.1, New Delhi: Dr. Ambedkar Foundation, 1979.

I

An Extraordinary Document

What is this extraordinary document?

The demand that India's political destiny should be determined by Indians themselves had been put forward by Mahatma Gandhi[1] as early as 1922, when freedom from British imperialism was still a distant dream. The failure of various grudging British attempts to devolve some elements of 'responsible self-governance' to satisfy Indian aspirations, accentuated the demand for a Constitution made by the people of India without outside interference, a demand officially asserted by the Indian National Congress in the 1920s.

But the process arguably has an older pedigree. Historically, no Indian was involved in the process of governance when the British Crown established its rule over India with the Government of India Act, 1858. Though Indians were gradually associated with governance through admission in modest numbers into the Indian Civil Service, they were initially given insignificant postings, usually in the rural districts, and denied involvement in significant constitutional affairs. In the twentieth century, the British began to delegate modest levels of authority to Indians

---

[1] Pankaja Srinivasan, 'Remembering Chauri Chaura and its impact on India's freedom movement', *The Hindu*, 14 August 2024.

through the Minto–Morley reforms of 1909, the Montagu–Chelmsford reforms of 1919 and finally the Government of India Act, 1935. The 'reforms' involved the very painfully slow eking out of constitutional authority into Indian hands through the delegation of limited powers over subsidiary issues. Though governance remained firmly in British hands, with the central government under the unchallengeable authority of the viceroy, they were depicted by the British as an effort aimed at 'the gradual development of self-governing institutions' in India.

Indians began demanding a greater say in their own governance with the establishment of the Indian National Congress in 1885. Decades of decorous petitioning of the British gave way to mass agitations during the Swadeshi movement beginning in 1905. Indian cooperation with the British war effort in World War I was premised on the assumption that the reward of Dominion Status for India would follow, but with the betrayal by perfidious Albion of such aspirations in the modest Montagu–Chelmsford reforms, nationalist agitation for constitutional change gathered pace. The non-cooperation movement, the Khilafat agitation, and other acts of civil disobedience led by Mahatma Gandhi propelled the nationalist movement towards greater demand for constitutional self-governance. This culminated in the first Indian attempt at drafting a Constitution in the late 1920s.

The Government of India Act, 1919, was meant to undergo a review after a decade, but the seven-member Simon Commission appointed to conduct the review was composed entirely of British officials. Angrily rejecting its composition and declaring non-cooperation with the Simon Commission, the Indian National Congress conducted an all-party conference in December 1927, which led to the creation of a committee chaired by Motilal Nehru to draft a Constitution for India. This led to the preparation in 1928 of the Motilal Nehru Report[2], drafted jointly by the Indian National Congress and several other parties, which outlined the key elements of such a Constitution.

The framers of the report rejected separate electorates based on religion, leading the Muslim League to reject the report. But its impact was significant. As the scholar widely considered the most authoritative external interpreter of the Constitution of India, Granville Austin,[3] observes in his seminal work *The Indian Constitution: Cornerstone of a Nation*, many of the trailblazing features of the Indian Constitution, such as universal adult franchise and a bouquet of unassailable rights, can be found in the Motilal Nehru Report. Ironically, it was only in the same year—1928—that our colonizers, the British, extended the vote to all women in their home island, while the United States, hailed as the world's oldest modern democracy, did not grant universal adult suffrage (which Independent India did from its very first election) until the Civil Rights Movement of the 1960s. These rights, in Austin's words, were 'a close precursor of the Fundamental Rights of the Constitution', because '10 of the 19 sub-clauses' reappear, materially unchanged, and three of the Nehru Report's rights are included in the Directive Principles of State Policy.[4] Hot on the heels of the Motilal Nehru Report came the Karachi Resolution[5] of the Indian

---

[2] 'Nehru Report (Motilal Nehru, 1928)', Constitution of India.
[3] Granville Austin, *The Indian Constitution: Cornerstone of a Nation*, Oxford: Clarendon Press, 1966, pp. xiii–iv.
[4] Ibid.
[5] 'Karachi Resolution 1931 (Indian National Congress)', Constitution of India.

National Congress in 1931, calling for full independence. In addition to reiterating the pioneering fundamental rights that were later to be incorporated into the Constitution, this resolution outlined a National Economic Programme—a litany which fuelled modern India's agrarian reforms and scripted her transition from a feudal to a modern society in the years immediately after Independence. With these precursors behind him, in 1938, Pandit Jawaharlal Nehru formulated this demand for a Constituent Assembly: 'The National Congress stands for independence and a democratic state. It has proposed that the Constitution of free India must be framed, without outside interference, by a Constituent Assembly, elected on the basis of adult franchise.'[6]

The draft Indian Constitution was adopted by the Constituent Assembly on 26 November 1949 and came into formal effect on 26 January 1950. At some 145,000 words[7], it was by far the longest written national Constitution in the world (for comparison, the US Constitution contains about 4,400 words, the French around 8,000, and the German, 20,000). Critics in the Constituent Assembly were cutting in their comments, finding the Constitution too long, not original enough and insufficiently Indian. Seth Govind Das expressed the trenchant view that the Constitution contained 'too many articles as also many details which could well have been left out'[8]. His Congress colleague K. Hanumanthaiah evocatively regretted that 'we wanted the music of veena or sitar, but here we have the music

---

[6] Durga Das Basu, *Introduction to the Constitution of India*, Calcutta: S. C. Sarkar, 1966, p. 14.
[7] Ananya Bhattacharya, 'India's constitution is 30 times longer than America's - and still growing', World Economic Forum, 2 October 2019.
[8] *Constituent Assembly Debates*, Vol. 11, 17 November 1949.

of an English band'[9]. Such views were echoed by critics outside the Assembly, notably (as we shall discuss later in the book) the Rashtriya Swayamsevak Sangh.

In 1950, the Indian Constitution consisted of 395 Articles (the individual provisions that outline specific laws, rights, duties, and procedures), 22 Parts (the broader divisions that group related Articles, helping organize the Constitution into coherent sections), and 8 Schedules (attached tables that provide additional details and information to support the Articles, such as allocation of powers between the union and states, and lists of recognized languages). At present, following the passage of 106 amendments, there are 448 Articles, 25 Parts, and 12 Schedules in the Constitution of India.[10]

The Preamble outlines the guiding principles of the Constitution, in the name of 'we the people of India'. Its text is succinct and powerful.

> WE, THE PEOPLE OF INDIA, having solemnly resolved to constitute India into a SOVEREIGN SOCIALIST SECULAR DEMOCRATIC REPUBLIC and to secure to all its citizens:
>
> JUSTICE, social, economic and political;
>
> LIBERTY of thought, expression, belief, faith and worship;
>
> EQUALITY of status and of opportunity; and to promote among them all
>
> FRATERNITY assuring the dignity of the individual

---

[9] Ibid.
[10] Rima Mondal, 'Analysis of Article 17 of the Indian Constitution', *Bn'W*, 10 October 2021.

and the unity and integrity of the Nation;

IN OUR CONSTITUENT ASSEMBLY this twenty-sixth day of November, 1949, do HEREBY ADOPT, ENACT AND GIVE TO OURSELVES THIS CONSTITUTION.

It is then followed by 22 Parts. These cover every conceivable topic of pertinent interest to the citizens of India (citizenship itself is defined in Part II) ranging from 'the Union and its Territory' (Part I, Articles 1–4) to 'the Panchayats' (Part IX) to 'Elections' (Part XV) and 'Official Language' (Part XVII). Part III of the Indian Constitution lays down the Fundamental Rights of the citizens of India; Articles 12 to 35 enumerate them. In particular, Articles 14 to 18 give all Indians the right to equality, ensuring that no person shall be discriminated against on the grounds of caste, sex, religion, race, or place of birth. Part IV lays down the Directive Principles of State Policy (Articles 36–51), an unusual feature of the Indian Constitution, which though not binding, offers guidance to the state on the principles to be applied in lawmaking in the future.

As Granville Austin observed, 'The Indian Constitution is first and foremost a social document. The majority of its provisions are either directly aimed at furthering the goals of the social revolution or attempt to foster this revolution by establishing the conditions necessary for its achievement.'[11] To Austin, the core of the commitment to the 'social revolution' lies in Parts III and IV, in the Fundamental Rights and in the Directive Principles of State Policy. These, he argues, are the conscience of the Constitution, and their roots lie in the struggle for Independence.

---

[11] Austin, *The Indian Constitution*, p. 50.

The Indian Constitution followed the example of the United States of America by enacting the equivalent of the American Bill of Rights. A wide range of fundamental rights have been granted to every Indian citizen, including the Right to Equality (Articles 14–18), the Right to Freedom (Articles 19–22), the Right against Exploitation (Articles 23–24), the Right to Freedom of Religion (Articles 25–28), Cultural and Educational Rights (Articles 29–30), and the Right to Constitutional Remedies (Article 32–35). The entire palette of rights can be enforced through the courts of law, from the lowliest sessions court all the way up to the Supreme Court of India. The judicially enforceable abolition of untouchability is a significant consequence of the establishment of these rights.

While the chapter on fundamental rights lays down what the state is prohibited from doing, such as discriminating against a citizen on the grounds of caste, or denying him the right to practise his religion, or suppressing her free speech, so too the chapter on directive principles sets out things which the state is encouraged to attempt to do, such as to provide free primary education, or grant public assistance in cases of unemployment, sickness or old age and more controversially, seek to establish a Uniform Civil Code (UCC, as suggested by Article 44) in a country riven by a variety of Personal Laws granted in British times to various communities. (We will examine the UCC issue later in the book.)

Unlike fundamental rights, however, the directive principles cannot be enforced through the courts of law, and serve as prescriptive precepts. According to Dr Ambedkar, the directives were meant to be the fundamental principles which should be made 'the basis of all the executive and legislative action'[12] in the future governance of the country. Some have been varyingly and inconsistently implemented by different states, such as the exhortation in Article 48 to 'organize agriculture and animal husbandry on modern and scientific lines and prohibit the slaughter of cows and calves and other milch and draught cattle'. Others have already made their way into federal legislation.

Despite their purely prescriptive nature, the directive principles have significantly influenced Indian policies and legislation, guiding successive governments in their efforts to bring about social change and create a more progressive state. In the arena of social and economic reforms, for instance, inspired by Articles 38 and 39, various land reform laws were enacted to redistribute land to the landless and ensure equitable distribution of resources: these have empowered tenant farmers, restricted large landholdings and abolished the feudal 'zamindari' system. Article 45 led to the enactment of the Right to Education Act, 2009, which makes education free and compulsory for children aged six to fourteen years: henceforth the onus is on the state and not just the parents to ensure that children are not out of school. Articles 41, 42, and 43 have influenced labour laws, ensuring better working conditions, maternity benefits, and fair wages (examples include the Minimum Wages Act, 1948, which Ambedkar himself fought for, and the Maternity Benefit Act, 1961). Article 40 led to the establishment of panchayati raj institutions through the Constitution (Seventy-third) Amendment Act, 1992, promoting local self-governance and giving more significant powers to village councils, affirming the principle that local problems were best dealt with by those

---

[12] *Constituent Assembly Debates*, Vol. VII, 19 November 1948.

closest to them. Article 48A has guided policies and laws aimed at environmental protection, such as the Environment Protection Act, 1986, and various initiatives for afforestation and wildlife conservation, which have notably given India a significant number of tiger reserves and enabled the revival of the species. Articles 46 and 335 have influenced policies for the upliftment of Scheduled Castes, Scheduled Tribes, and Other Backward Classes, including reservation in education and employment in ways that have transformed millions of lives. Article 39A led to the establishment of the National Legal Services Authority (NALSA) to provide free legal aid to the underprivileged, all the more essential in a land of widespread illiteracy. Article 47 has driven policies to improve public health, such as the National Health Mission and various vaccination programmes. Articles 41 and 43 have influenced the creation of social security schemes like the Mahatma Gandhi National Rural Employment Guarantee Act (MGNREGA), which provides a hundred days' guaranteed employment to at least one member of every rural household living below the poverty line. These examples demonstrate that the directive principles have thus played a crucial role in shaping India's socio-economic landscape, guiding the government towards achieving a more equitable and just society. They continue to serve as a moral compass for policymakers.

While the idea of fundamental rights is deeply entrenched in constitutional doctrines around the world, the French Revolution Constitution of 1795 and the Mexican Cadiz Constitution of 1812 were unusual in containing also a list of duties enjoined upon the citizen. As Mahatma Gandhi wrote in 1947, 'I learned from my illiterate but wise mother that all rights to be deserved and preserved, come from duty well done. Thus, the very right to live accrues to us only when we do the duty of citizenship of the world. From this one fundamental statement, perhaps it is easy enough to define the duties of man and woman and correlate every right to some corresponding duty to be first performed.' In a letter to H. G. Wells, who had embarked upon drafting a universal bill of rights, Gandhi suggested instead: 'Begin with a charter of Duties of Man, and I promise the rights will follow as spring follows winter. I write from experience.... I began by discovering and performing my duty by my wife, my children, my friends, companions, and society, and I find today that I have greater rights perhaps than any living man I know.'

Gandhi did not have his way when the Constitution was drafted. It was only thirty-eight years after his death, in 1976, that a list of fundamental duties was incorporated into the Constitution, when the Forty-second Amendment was inserted in Part IVA, Article 51A, incorporating ten fundamental duties, ranging from respecting the Constitution and upholding sovereignty to somewhat vaguer goals like valuing heritage, striving for excellence, and developing a scientific temper. An eleventh was added in 2004, urging parents to provide opportunities for education to their children between the ages of six and fourteen. If the fundamental rights are judicially enforceable and the directive principles prescriptive, the 'fundamental duties' may be said to be essentially exhortatory. It is hard to imagine anyone being prosecuted for failing to fulfil a fundamental duty, let alone a court taking cognizance of such an offence.

National unity was a vital preoccupation of the Constitution-makers, particularly in the wake of the savage vivisection of the country by Partition. This accounts for the centralizing tendencies embedded in the Constitution, which tilt India's federalism clearly towards the national executive. The founders' concern for national unity emerged as the central issue during the framing of the federal and language provisions as well as in the inclusion of the Emergency Provisions (Part XVIII, Articles 352 to 360) which allows for the suspension of specific rights and gives sweeping authority to the centre in the name of domestic stability—during crises like war, state failure, or financial turbulence. Legislative powers in the Constitution are divided between the centre and states (Part XI, Articles 245 to 263). This division extends to both territorial limits and topics of legislation—elaborated in the three lists of the Seventh Schedule—Union, State, and Concurrent. As such, the Constitution envisages a federation, but one modelled more on Canada's rather than the American or Australian federations, in that the powers not allocated to the units belong, as in Canada, to the centre, whereas in Australia and the US the powers not granted to the centre remain with the federating states. Again, like Canada, the Indian Constitution includes provisions relating not only to the union, but also to the constituent states, whereas the Constitutions of Australia and of the US deal with the national government but barely touch upon the states.[13]

There are, nonetheless, distinctive Indian features to the Constitution not found in these models but dictated by the tumultuous circumstances of the country's birth as a constitutional republic. Through its very first amendment, the Constitution stopped short of granting Indians the absolute right to freedom of speech and expression, deciding that

---

[13] B. N. Rau, 'The Indian Constitution', *India Quarterly*, Vol. 5, No. 4, October–November 1949, pp. 293–303.

'reasonable restrictions' could be imposed on grounds of public order, decency, morality, defamation and, even, friendly relations with foreign states. The First Amendment, enacted in 1951, introduced these new grounds for restricting freedom of speech and expression, in order to protect laws related to public safety, press regulations, and criminal provisions from being struck down by the judiciary. It also protected specific sections of the Indian Penal Code (IPC) from being declared unconstitutional, including laws related to sedition, promoting enmity between different groups, and deliberate acts intended to outrage religious feelings. These changes were introduced to address judicial decisions that had struck down provisions of public safety laws and other regulations which were seen as incompatible with the constitutional right to freedom of speech and expression, but which the government deemed essential to promote its social agenda and maintain peace in a strife-torn land just years after the country's violent Partition. By curbing freedom of speech in the interests of state security, creating a special schedule of unconstitutional laws immune to judicial review, and imposing restrictions on the right to property and freedom from discrimination, the First Amendment arguably created a wholly new relationship between the citizen and the state.[14] But it was passed by the very makers of the Constitution themselves, who had served in the Constituent Assembly before its conversion the previous year into a Parliament, and so cannot be deemed to have departed from the 'original intent' of the founders.

The Constitution-makers—who included fifteen women, 5 per cent of the membership—were not working in a

---

[14] Tripurdaman Singh, *Sixteen Stormy Days: The Story of the First Amendment of the Constitution of India*, New Delhi: Bloomsbury Publishing, 2020.

vacuum: even as their labours went on, the nation was grappling with issues like food shortages, communal riots, communist subversion, and forced migration, while events abroad during those turbulent years included wars, upheavals, and the overthrow of governments. (Despite their modest number, the women members made significant contributions to the Assembly's debates on such vital issues as women's rights, female education, health and social reforms, and the rights of the Depressed Classes, and participated effectively in debates on the principle of equality, separate electorates, and local government autonomy.)

The fact that the Constitution of India has recently celebrated its seventy-fifth birthday is no insignificant achievement. The French have had over a dozen Constitutions between 1791 and 1958, when the fifth republic was created. Mexico had four Constitutions in the century from 1824, while Argentina and Brazil had five each between the mid-nineteenth and late-twentieth centuries. Nepal had six Constitutions between 1948 and 2007 and still rewrote a seventh one in 2015. By comparison, India retained its constitutional framework for three-quarters of a century even while making multiple amendments.

The Constitution was created during a time of turbulence and tumult as a document that would draw from the past but deal effectively with the challenges of the present. Yet the drafters trained their aspirations on setting high standards for themselves and their nation. As Granville Austin, who authored the first definitive study of the working of the Constituent Assembly, observed:

> The Indians' sense of their rich cultural heritage, their record of professional achievement in the arts and

sciences of the modern world, and their faith in their ability to govern themselves, combined to give them a national maturity that allowed a reasoned approach to the creation and working of government. Equipped with the basic qualifications, attitudes, and experience for creating and working a democratic constitution, Indians did not default their tryst with destiny.[15]

---

[15] Austin, *The Indian Constitution*, p. 330.

II

The Vision of the Founders

The context behind the Constitution's adoption was the world's first major triumph of decolonization in the twentieth century, the birth of India as a free nation from the ashes of the British Raj. At midnight on 15 August 1947, independent India was born. Its first prime minister, Jawaharlal Nehru, described the hour as 'a tryst with destiny...a moment... which comes but rarely in history, when we step out from the old to the new, when an age ends, and when the soul of a nation, long suppressed, finds utterance.' With those words he launched India on a remarkable journey—remarkable because it was happening at all. 'India,' Winston Churchill had once snarled, 'is merely a geographical expression. It is no more a single country than the Equator.' Although Churchill was often wrong about India, it is true that no other country in the world embraces the extraordinary mixture of ethnic groups, profusion of mutually incomprehensible languages, varieties of topography and climate, diversity of religions and cultural practices, and range of levels of economic development that India does. Could a united nation be welded from such a congeries, and what kind of Constitution could hope to hold it together while enabling progress and social transformation in an environment of freedom, human rights, and personal liberty?

Many would have argued that the task was impossible—that India was too riven by contradictions to be considered one country at all. Those contradictions were repeatedly stressed by British rulers in self-justification for their rule. Like Churchill, the British statesman and writer Benjamin Disraeli (who memorably said that 'a nation is a work of art and a work of time', gradually created by a variety of influences, including climate, soil, religion, customs, manners, historical incidents and accidents, and so on, which 'form the national mind'), argued that India was not a nation: it lacked a common language, a common religion, a shared tradition, a historical experience, a cohesive majority, and a defined territory, all of which he regarded as the essential ingredients of a nation. But Indian nationalists had an effective riposte. India is a country held together, in the words of Nehru, 'by strong but invisible threads...a myth and an idea, a dream and a vision, and yet very real and present and pervasive.'[1]

The challenge of defining India is immense. It is a land of snow peaks and tropical jungles, with twenty-two major languages (listed in the Constitution)[2] and over 20,000 distinct 'dialects' (including some of which are spoken by more people than Swedish, Maori, or Estonian), inhabited in the middle of the third decade of the twenty-first century by more than 1.4 billion individuals of almost every ethnic extraction known to humanity. It has given birth to four major religions and offers a home to many more; it preaches doctrines of spirituality and wisdom, anchored in

---

[1] Jawaharlal Nehru, *The Discovery of India*, Calcutta: Signet Press, 1946.
[2] 'Languages Included in the Eighth Schedule of the Indian Constitution', Government of India, Department of Official Language.

universalism and inclusivity, while still being afflicted by a caste system that visits grave disabilities upon millions of its people. It has two major classical music traditions (Carnatic and Hindustani) to go with innumerable folk disciplines; multiple classical dance forms (Kathakali, Kuchipudi, Bharata Natyam, Kathak, Manipuri, Odissi, and so on) that create a rich jambalaya of diverse cultures transmitted through gurus directly mentoring select students; and by far the largest film industry in the world. In the phrase of the American poet Walt Whitman, it is vast; it contains multitudes.

And yet, the notion of Bharatvarsha in the Rig Veda, of a land stretching from the Himalaya to the seas, contained the original territorial notion of India; for the bounds imposed by the mountains and the oceans created common bonds as well, making the conception of India as one civilization inhabiting a coherent territorial space and a shared history truly timeless. There are deep continuities, therefore, in the imagining of Indian nationhood, which transcend centuries of internal division.

Even if 'nationalism' as a concept arose in Europe in the nineteenth century, people everywhere had a sense of belonging to communities larger than themselves: after all, the notion of the Muslim ummah, or the Vedanta philosopher Adi Shankaracharya's conception of Hinduism's sacred geography, both imply large communities that people could identify with. In this sense it is not contradictory to argue that India is an 'old' nation, even though 'nation' is a new concept. But the nation became a salient political category in India only with the anti-colonial struggle, the case for collective self-government, and the dawn of democracy. So long as India was governed by monarchs or empires, Indians were subjects, and the question of identification was often more cultural than political. As Indians became citizens, the story changed.

But the framers of the Constitution had to take the traditional idea of India and anchor it in a Constitution to create a modern nation based on a certain conception of human rights and citizenship, vigorously backed by a spirit of fraternity, and equality before the law. Earlier conceptions of India drew their inspiration from mythology and theology. The modern idea of India, despite the mystical influence of the Nobel Prize-winning poet Rabindranath Tagore, and the spiritual and moral influences of Mahatma Gandhi, is a robustly secular and legal construct based upon the vision and intellect of our Founding Fathers, notably (in alphabetical order!) Ambedkar, Nehru, and Sardar Vallabhbhai Patel. Ambedkar, born an 'untouchable' (Dalit), a brilliant intellectual with degrees in economics and law from the finest US and British universities, envisioned a society based on equality, justice, and liberty. He emphasized the importance of constitutional democracy, the rule of law, and the protection of individual rights, aiming to eradicate social inequalities, particularly untouchability, and to 'annihilate' the caste system. The patrician Nehru, born a child of privilege, rose to the pinnacle of the nationalist movement with a vision to build a secular, democratic, and industrialized India. He championed parliamentary democracy, secularism, and socialism, focusing on economic development through state intervention and planning, and seeing the Constitution as an instrument of social and economic transformation. Patel, a doughty lawyer from farming stock, a steel-willed organizer and convinced Gandhian, shared few of the ideological views of the other two. His vision centred on national unity and strong governance, administrative efficiency and national security; with tough pragmatism, he played a crucial role in integrating the 565 'princely states' into the Indian union. All three men converged on the core objectives of the Constitution: to constitute a nation, ensure its democracy, and enable its social and economic development. The Preamble of the Constitution itself is the most eloquent enumeration of their shared vision. In its description of the defining traits of the Indian republic, and its conception of justice, of liberty, of equality and fraternity, it firmly establishes the basis of the national project.

The role of liberal constitutionalism in shaping and undergirding the civic nationalism of India is the dominant strand in the broader story of the evolution and modernization of Indian society, especially over the last century. The principal task of any Constitution is to constitute: that is, to define the rules, the shared norms, values and systems under which the state will function and the nation will evolve. Every society has an interdependent relationship with the legal systems that govern it, which is both complex and, especially in our turbulent times, continuously and vociferously contested. It is through this interplay that communities become societies, societies become civilizations, and civilizations acquire a sense of national and historical character.

The chairman of the Drafting Committee of the Constituent Assembly, Dr B. R. Ambedkar, would no doubt have argued that the constitutional roots of Indian republicanism ran deep. He remarked that some ancient Indian states were republics, notably those of the Licchavis who ruled northern Bihar and lower Nepal in the sixth and fifth centuries BCE (around the Buddha's time), the Mallas, centred in the city of Kushinagara, and the Vajji (or Vriji) confederation, based in the city of Vaishali. Early Indian republicanism can be traced back to the independent gana sanghas, which appear to have existed between the sixth and fourth centuries BCE. The Greek historian Diodorus Siculus, describing India at the time of Alexander the Great's invasion in 326 BCE (though he was writing two centuries later), recorded that independent and democratic republics existed in India.[3] They seemed, however, to include a monarch or raja, and a deliberative assembly that met regularly and discussed all major state decisions. The gana sanghas had full financial, administrative, and judicial authority and elected the raja, who therefore was not a hereditary monarch. The raja reported to the assembly and in some states, was assisted by a council of other nobles.

The oldest Indian republics varied in their constitutional arrangements. The Licchavis had a primary governing body of 7,077 heads of the most important families in the republic, while the Shakyas, Koliyas, and Mallas opened their assembly to the participation of all men, rich and poor. Villages had their own assemblies, under local chiefs called gramakas. But despite the assemblies, it is not entirely clear whether the composition and participation were truly popular, and the unequal caste duties and privileges of the members might well have affected their roles in the state, whatever be the formal importance of the institutions. Still, in the absence of hereditary monarchs with absolute powers, these states allow India to claim a standing equal to that of ancient Greece or Rome in the evolutionary history of the republic. It is no surprise, then, that while the ancient and

---

[3] Diodorus Siculus, *Bibliotheca Historica*, Vol. II., translated by C. H. Oldfather, Library of History: Loeb Classical Library, Cambridge: Harvard University Press, 1935.

medieval worlds largely celebrated kings and conquerors, India, while generally observing the same traditions, had other inspirations to hark back to before it entered the era of monarchs and emperors. The early Indian polities had systems, edicts, and policies, but not legislation in the sense we would understand the term today. But these traditions largely lapsed in the long interregnum of Muslim rule, when the alternative to an Islamist imperium was usually one of an assortment of Hindu monarchs, and neither democracy nor rule of law flourished anywhere in the subcontinent.

The British interlude was undoubtedly transformative, and it helped introduce the idea of 'the law' as the guiding principle of government, and therefore, implicitly (when one came into being) of the state. With the advent of the law, lawyers naturally rose to prominence in affairs of state. Since the Age of Enlightenment (also called the 'Age of Reason', when European politics, philosophy, science and communications were radically reoriented from 1685–1815), many of the great people who changed the course of their nations, and the world, for good, and sometimes for the worse, have been lawyers. India was no exception: in the Constituent Assembly Ambedkar, Nehru, and Patel were all lawyers (as were the principal progenitors of the subcontinent's two nationalisms before Independence, Mahatma Gandhi and Mohammed Ali Jinnah, the erstwhile Congressman who would go on to lead the Muslim League and then Pakistan). These men, and the fifteen impressive women who joined them, had the vision and the intellect to anticipate the problems and challenges that all civilizations in the modern era have had to confront. Though elected by the limited franchise permitted by the British in their rationing of democratic freedoms to Indians, the members of the Constituent Assembly, across all political lines and backgrounds, enjoyed great legitimacy, particularly those whose leadership of the freedom struggle had entailed great personal commitment and sacrifice. In the process, these distinguished lawyers found the best check-and-balance mechanism in the political and legal system created by and reflected in, the Constitution, to combat these challenges and to protect the interests of all Indians in equal measure.

In dealing with the vast and complex realities of a subcontinent of (at that time) 330 million people, politically administered in a dozen different administrative units, while seeking to integrate 565 'princely states' into the new republic, and in devising systems and rules to embrace all of them, the founders had to acknowledge the need to produce political unity out of ethnic, religious, cultural, linguistic, and communal diversity. As I have often argued, the most viable approach to India lies in a simple insight—the singular thing about India is that you can only speak of it in the plural. There are, in the hackneyed phrase, many Indias. Everything exists in countless variants. There is no single standard, no fixed stereotype, no 'one way'. Throughout the first seven decades of Independence, India's pluralism was acknowledged in its constitutional and political arrangements, which encouraged a bewildering variety of social groups, religious communities, sectional interests, and far-fetched ideologies to flourish and contend. Even though India was partitioned when the British carved chunks out of it to create a homeland for its Muslims, it embraced the Muslims who remained (for several decades there were more Muslims in India than in Pakistan), and sustained them through an official policy of secularism that is now bitterly challenged by its current ruling party. In an era when most developing countries chose authoritarian models of government, claiming these were needed to promote nation-building and to steer economic development, India chose to be a multi-party democracy. And despite many ups and downs, and moments of greater or lesser stress on its democratic institutions (of which more later in the book), India has remained a democracy—flawed, perhaps, but flourishing.

Many observers abroad have been astonished by India's survival as a pluralist state. But India could hardly have survived as anything else. Pluralism is a reality that emerges from the very nature of the country; it is a choice made inevitable by India's geography and reaffirmed by its history.

Pluralism and inclusiveness have long marked the essence of India. India's is a civilization that, over millennia, has offered refuge and, more importantly, religious and cultural freedom, to Jews, Parsis, several denominations of Christians, and, of course, Muslims. Jews came to Kerala centuries before Christ, with the destruction by the Babylonians of their First Temple, and they knew no persecution on Indian soil until the Portuguese arrived in the sixteenth century to inflict it. Christianity arrived on Indian soil with St Thomas the Apostle (the Doubting Thomas of biblical lore), who came to the Kerala coast some time before 52 CE and was welcomed onshore, if legend is to be believed, by a flute-playing Jewish girl. He converted many to his faith, so there are Indians today whose ancestors were Christian well before any Europeans discovered Christianity. Islam is portrayed by some in the north as a religion of invaders who pillaged and conquered, but in Kerala, where Islam came through traders, travellers, and preachers rather than by the sword, a south Indian king was so impressed by the message of the Prophet that he travelled to Arabia to meet the great teacher himself. The king, Cheraman Perumal, perished in the attempt, but the Kerala coconuts he took with him have sprouted trees that flourish to this day on the southern coast of Oman. Indeed, the Zamorin of Calicut was so impressed by the seafaring skills of the Muslim community (epitomized in the famed and fearless Kunjali Marikkars) that he issued a decree obliging each fisherman's family to bring up one son as a Muslim to man his all-Muslim navy!

India's heritage of diversity means that in the Kolkata neighbourhood where I lived during my high school years, the wail of the muezzin calling the Islamic faithful to prayer routinely blended with the chant of mantras and the tinkling of bells at the local Shiva temple, accompanied by the Sikh gurdwara's reading of verses from the Guru Granth Sahib, with St. Paul's Cathedral just around the corner. Today, I represent in the national Parliament the constituency of Thiruvananthapuram, the capital of Kerala, where the gleaming white dome of the Palayam Juma Masjid stands diagonally across from the lofty spires of St. Joseph's Cathedral, and just around the corner from both, abutting the mosque, is one of the city's oldest temples, consecrated to Lord Ganesha and recently renovated. My experiences and encounters in my constituency remind me daily that India is home to more Christians than Australia and nearly as many Muslims as Pakistan.

That is the India the Constitution seeks to reify.

III

The Constitution and Indian Nationhood

The very idea of India is therefore of one land embracing many. It is the idea that a nation may accommodate—indeed, celebrate—differences of caste, creed, colour, culture, cuisine, conviction, costume, and custom, and still rally around a democratic consensus. That consensus is around the simple constitutional principle that in a democracy under the rule of law, you do not really need to agree all the time—except on the ground rules of how you will disagree. The reason India has survived all the stresses and strains that have beset it for nearly eight decades, and that led so many to predict its imminent disintegration, is that it maintained consensus on how to manage without consensus. Today, those in positions of power seem to be scorning these ground rules, which are enshrined, alongside the idea of India, in our Constitution. This is why it is imperative, today more than ever, to reaffirm those rules, that idea, and—above all—our Constitution.

The Constitution had to incorporate, in its very essence, this idea of Indian nationhood, which had emerged from the nationalist movement. Nationalism, to my mind, is essentially divisible into those forms that are changeless (like ethnicity and identity-based nationalism) and those where the sense of nationhood inheres in institutions, practices, and systems enshrined in a Constitution and reaffirmed regularly through a democratic vote—in other words, civic nationalism. Whereas ethnic nationhood inheres in the body, civic nationalism appeals to the mind; it is a nationalism of constitutions and institutions you respect, rather than identities you are born into. In using 'ethnic nationalism' as shorthand for what most people traditionally understand by the idea of nationalism, I admit, of course, that nationalism always goes a step further than mere ethnocentrism, in that it seeks and demands loyalty to a politically distinct entity, requires membership in an organized mass social group or community, insists on fealty to a formalized ideology, and requires of its adherents the performance of certain actions or behaviours to confirm their allegiance to the nation, such as saluting the flag, singing the anthem, or swearing loyalty to the state. Still, if its basis is the unchanging qualities one largely acquires by the accidental circumstance of birth, it falls into the category of 'classic' ethnic nationalism. Civic nationalism, while still nationalist, is distinguished from ethnic nationalism by the very fact that ethnicity and its trappings are irrelevant to a nationalist's sense of allegiance to his country. It is this latter idea that the Constitution of India implicitly incorporated.

Civic nationalism is a concept that drives those states that derive their political legitimacy not from ethnicity, religion, language, culture, or any of the immutable trappings that people acquire from birth, but from the consent and active participation of their citizens, as free members of a democratic polity. Ideas of civic nationalism are said to have originated from the writings of European philosophers like John Locke and Jean-Jacques Rousseau, and especially with the latter's 1762 book, *The Social Contract*, which describes the legitimacy of government being derived from the 'general will' of the people. Membership of the civic nation is voluntary and can be acquired not only by birth but by immigration and usually (except in a handful of countries) renunciation of other allegiances. Civic nationalism requires liberal democratic institutions, constitutionalism that guarantees freedom of speech and association, and representative democracy, and is therefore the form of nationalism most closely associated with the modern state. Since these essential attributes are not totally inconsistent with the majoritarian impulse prevalent in ethno-nationalist 'illiberal democracies', civic nationalism rests on liberal constitutionalism to prevent such distortions. While the United States of America and France are often described as prototypes of civic nationalism, anti-colonial nationalism like India's evolved into civic nationalism, and, arguably, a once ethnic nationalism like Germany's has been transformed into the same variant today.

Indian civic nationalism thus required allegiance to an idea of India transcending religious, ethnic, linguistic, and other sub-national identities. 'I do not want that our loyalty as Indians should be in the slightest way affected by any competitive loyalty,' said Ambedkar, 'whether that loyalty arises out of our religion, out of our culture or out of our language. I want all people to be Indians first, Indians last and nothing else but Indians.'[1] He was explicitly rejecting the divisions by religion, caste, region, and language which the likes of Churchill would have seen as definitive. The Constitution set about formally and legally establishing who 'Indians' were.

---

[1] Speech to the Bombay Assembly, quoted in Irfan S. Habib (ed.), *Indian Nationalism: The Essential Writings*, New Delhi: Aleph Book Company, 2017, p. 27.

In doing so, and in their attempt to give the country the best Constitution they could, its framers borrowed from and were inspired by models from around the world. The structure of Parliament, including the roles of the Lok Sabha (House of the People) and the Rajya Sabha (Council of States), and concept of a cabinet system of government, where the executive is responsible to the legislature, were inspired by the British system. The idea of a written Constitution and the inclusion of a Bill of Rights, along with the concept of judicial review, allowing the judiciary to strike down laws that violate the Constitution, were inspired by the US Constitution. The words 'equal protection of the laws'[2] in Article 14 were taken from the Fourteenth Amendment to the US Constitution. The exceptions to the freedom of speech and expression incorporated in Article 19(2) were included in emulation of the Irish Constitution. The phrase 'procedure established by law'[3] in Article 21 was borrowed from Article 31 of the Japanese Constitution. The Directive Principles of State Policy, as we have seen, were inspired by the Irish Constitution. The concept of a strong central government with a federal structure, in which powers are divided between the central and state governments, was influenced by the Canadian model. The idea of emergency provisions, allowing the central government to take control during times of crisis, was inspired by the Weimar Constitution of Germany. The concept of concurrent powers, where both the central and state governments can legislate on certain subjects, was borrowed from the Australian Constitution.

---

[2] '14th Amendment to the U.S. Constitution: Civil Rights (1868)', National Archives.
[3] 'The Constitution of Japan', Prime Minister's Office of Japan.

And the principles of liberty, equality, and fraternity, which are enshrined in the Preamble of the Indian Constitution, were inspired by the French Revolution.

This did not sit well with some nationalist members of the Constituent Assembly. As early as 30 August 1947, a member of the Assembly, P. S. Deshmukh,[4] deplored that India seemed to be borrowing its Constitution from those of Ireland and the British Raj's Government of India Act. Such charges continued to be laid over the following year of deliberations, prompting Ambedkar to respond, while presenting a first draft in November 1948:

> It is said that there is nothing new in the Draft Constitution, that about half of it has been copied from the Government of India Act of 1935 and that the rest of it has been borrowed from the Constitutions of other countries. Very little of it can claim originality. One likes to ask whether there can be anything new in a Constitution framed at this hour in the history of the world. More than hundred years have rolled over when the first written Constitution was drafted. It has been followed by many countries reducing their Constitutions to writing. What the scope of a Constitution should be has long been settled. Similarly, what are the fundamentals of a Constitution are recognized all over the world. Given these facts, all Constitutions in their main provisions must look similar.[5]

---

[4] Vineeth Krishna, 'B.R. Ambedkar's Defence of Constitutional Borrowing', Constitution of India.
[5] Ibid.

Having acknowledged and justified this seeming lack of originality, Ambedkar then proceeded to explain why it was unfair to view the Indian version as entirely borrowed.

> The only new things, if there can be any, in a Constitution framed so late in the day are the variations made to remove the faults and to accommodate it to the needs of the country. The charge of producing a blind copy of the Constitutions of other countries is based, I am sure, on an inadequate study of the Constitution. I have shown what is new in the Draft Constitution and I am sure that those who have studied other Constitutions and who are prepared to consider the matter dispassionately will agree that the Drafting Committee in performing its duty has not been guilty of such blind and slavish imitation as it is represented to be.[6]

'I make no apologies', he added, because '[t]here is nothing to be ashamed of in borrowing. It involves no plagiarism. Nobody holds any patent rights in the fundamental ideas of a constitution.'[7] Still, he was right in claiming to have 'accommodated' external ideas to the 'needs of the country'. In Article 21, for example, the Constitution avoided the American phrase 'due process of law' because the drafters were aware that the US Supreme Court had used this language to strike down social welfare legislation during the Great Depression, and they did not want to give Indian courts the same power. Similarly, the exceptions to free speech

---

[6] Ibid.
[7] 'Dr. B.R. Ambedkar's speech introducing the Draft Constitution in the Constituent Assembly on Nov. 04, 1948', *B. R. Ambedkar Selected Speeches*, Prasar Bharati.

enumerated in Article 19(2), though the idea was inspired by the Irish Constitution, included the words 'friendly relations with foreign states' in the Indian Constitution in order to restrict the right to advocate, as some were doing, the forcible reintegration of Pakistan into India.[8]

Jawaharlal Nehru's opening remarks when he moved the motion at the newly established Constituent Assembly on 13 December 1946 gives us a sense of the immense pressure and responsibility on the lawmakers to ensure that they responded fittingly to the situation and did justice to the task of Constitution-making. They were conscious they had to preserve the essential past while marching towards the future. Nehru said:

> We are at the end of an era and possibly very soon we shall embark upon a new age; and my mind goes back to the great past of India, to the 5,000 years of India's history, from the very dawn of that history which might be considered almost the dawn of human history, till today. All that past crowds around me and exhilarates me and, at the same time, somewhat oppresses me. Am I worthy of that past? When I think also of the future, the greater future I hope, standing on this sword's edge of the present between this mighty past and the mightier future, I tremble a little and feel overwhelmed by this mighty task.[9]

Dr Ambedkar's concluding remarks to the Constituent Assembly in the 'The Grammar of Anarchy' speech he gave

---

[8] Abhinav Chandrachud, 'Why India's Constitution still thrives after 75 years of scrutiny', *Indian Express*, 5 February 2025.
[9] Jawaharlal Nehru, *Words of Freedom: Ideas of a Nation*, New Delhi: Penguin Books, 2010.

on 25 November 1949 offered a fitting coda. He spoke of the maladies of India and its ideal state, to be ensured by the rule of law. In a magisterial expression of India through the prism of politics, law, and social hierarchies, he highlighted the fact that 'there is complete absence of two things in Indian society'—equality and fraternity. 'On the 26th of January 1950,' he declared, 'we are going to enter into a life of contradictions. In politics we will be recognizing the principle of one man one vote and one vote one value. In our social and economic life, we shall, by reason of our social and economic structure, continue to deny the principle of one man one value. How long shall we continue to live this life of contradictions? How long shall we continue to deny equality in our social and economic life?'[10]

In calling for a social and not merely political democracy to emerge from the Constitution, Ambedkar stressed the absence of fraternity as the second major ingredient that was missing in India. 'Fraternity means a sense of common brotherhood of all Indians—of Indians being one people. It is the principle which gives unity and solidarity to social life.'[11] But thanks to the caste system—the entire structure of caste, he averred, was 'anti-national'—religious divisions and the absence of a sense of nationhood among some Indians, fraternity had not yet been achieved. But it was indispensable, since liberty, equality, and fraternity were all intertwined and could not flourish independently of one another. 'Without equality,' he pointed out, 'liberty would produce the supremacy of the few over the many. Equality

---

[10] B. R. Ambedkar, 'The Grammar of Anarchy', Speech to the Constituent Assembly, 25 November 1949.
[11] Ibid.

without liberty would kill individual initiative. Without fraternity, liberty would produce the supremacy of the few over the many. Without fraternity, liberty and equality could not become a natural course of things. It would require a constable to enforce them.'[12]

Ambedkar's eloquent assault on discrimination and untouchability, for the first time, cogently expanded the reach of the Indian idea to incorporate the nation's vast, neglected underclass. Ambedkar—a product of Columbia University and the London School of Economics, and the first Indian principal of the prestigious Government Law College in Bombay—was deeply troubled by the iniquities of the caste system and the fear of many Dalits that national independence would merely lead to the social and political dominance of the upper castes. As an opponent of caste, and a nationalist, he believed that the Dalits must support India's freedom from British rule but they must pursue their struggle for equal rights within the framework of the new Constitution that he had a major hand in drafting.

Today, over seventy-five years later, it is well worth asking what progress we have made to achieve the aims of the Constitution's drafters, and in particular to fill the lacunae that Ambedkar identified. Equality has advanced, no doubt, with the abolition of untouchability being accompanied by the world's oldest and farthest-reaching affirmative action programme, in the form of reservations, initially for Scheduled Castes and then for the Other Backward Classes. These reservations, which were initially intended to be temporary, have now been entrenched in our system and may be said

---

[12] Ibid.

to be politically unchallengeable. But the task of promoting social and economic equality, which Ambedkar pointed to, is far from complete. The clamour for further opportunities for those who believe that Indian society continues to deny them the equality of outcomes that their numbers warrant, continues to roil our politics. The escalating demand for a caste census is bound to have further implications for the evolution of India's constitutional practice.

As for fraternity, the mobilization of votes in our contentious democracy in the name of caste, creed, region, and language have ensured that the social and psychological sense of oneness that Ambedkar spoke about is still, at best, a work in progress. But there is no doubt that the sense of nationhood—that he felt had not yet come into existence—has now become embedded across the country. One only needs to look at the crowds at a cricket match involving the Indian team, or the national mourning after an international conflict like the Kargil War of 1999 or the Galwan incident of 2020, to be aware that there is a strong sense of nationhood despite the persistence of local or sectarian identities.

Yet, by entrenching caste reservations, India has promoted equality but arguably undermined fraternity. Fraternity had a special place in Ambedkar's vision; the word was, in many ways, his distinctive contribution to India's constitutional discourse. It also had an economic dimension, with the implicit idea that the assets of the better-off would be used to uplift the untouchables and other unfortunates. Fraternity would both result from and lead to the erosion of social and caste hierarchies. But, as the sociologist Dipankar Gupta has argued,[13] the extension of reservations to the Other Backward Classes saw caste as 'an important political resource to be plumbed in perpetuity'. Gupta avers that this 'is not in the spirit of enlarging fraternity, as the Ambedkar proposals are; while Ambedkar's ultimate aim was the annihilation of caste from Indian society, for Mandal, caste was not to be "removed", but to be "represented".' It entrenched caste rather than eliminating it from public life.

---

[13] Dipankar Gupta, 'Positive Discrimination and the Question of Fraternity: Contrasting Ambedkar and Mandal on Reservations', *Economic and Political Weekly*, Vol. 32, No. 31, 1997, pp. 1971–78.

IV

Elements of the Constitution

Ambedkar stressed in the Constituent Assembly that the Constitution was the working instrument of our democracy. It creates the basic framework of our democracy, including the three main organs of the state—the legislature, the executive, and the judiciary. The Constitution defines their powers, delimits their jurisdictions, demarcates their responsibilities, and regulates their relationships with one another, and with the people. But the most important contribution of the Constitution to Indian civic nationalism was that of representation centred on individuals. As the legal scholar Madhav Khosla explains in his impressive book of legal history, *India's Founding Moment: The Constitution of a Most Surprising Democracy*, the political apparatus of establishing a constitutional democracy in postcolonial India—a land that was 'poor and illiterate; divided by caste, religion, and languages; and burdened by centuries of tradition',[1] involved an attempt to free Indians from prevailing types of knowledge and understanding, to place citizens in a realm of individual agency and deliberation that was appropriate to self-rule and to alter the relationship that they shared with one another.

---

[1] Madhav Khosla, *India's Founding Moment: The Constitution of a Most Surprising Democracy*, Cambridge: Harvard University Press, 2019, p. 6.

The founders of the republic chose to impose a liberal Constitution upon a decidedly illiberal society, hidebound as it was by traditional customs and entrenched prejudices relating to caste, religion, and social hierarchies. They saw the principles of liberal constitutionalism—the centrality of the state, non-communal political representation, and so on—as responsive to the challenges posed by the burden of democracy. In keeping with contemporary liberal thought, they committed India to a common language of the rule of law, constructed a centralized state, rejected localism, and instituted a model of representation whose units were individuals rather than groups.

It is particularly striking, when examined in today's context, that the Constitution-makers explicitly rejected the notion of religion playing any role in citizenship, arguing that each individual voter exercised agency in the democratic project and should not be reduced to the pre-existing loyalties of religious affiliation. 'For India's founders,' Khosla observes, 'one could not be a political agent unless one's political identity was self-created.'[2] The Constitution granted representation not to one's predetermined identity (religion or caste) but to one's individual expression of agency. That was why the individual vote was so important. Democratic politics could not be reduced to the advocacy of preset interests derived from one's identity at birth; interests instead had to be expressed through politics. 'The very constitution of one's identity as a citizen,' Khosla explains, 'was itself a form of freedom.'[3]

It is also striking that the Constituent Assembly rejected

---

[2] Khosla, *India's Founding Moment*, p. 137.
[3] Ibid., p. 140.

separate electorates, weighted representation, and reservations on the basis of religion. Only days before Indian Independence, and the Partition of British India, Sardar Vallabhbhai Patel, in his capacity as chairman of the Advisory Committee on Minorities and Fundamental Rights, wrote to the president of the Assembly, Rajendra Prasad, to explain why separate electorates had been rejected. Differentiated citizenship on the basis of religion, Patel argued, had already been tried in the colonial era and had led to Partition. The answer lay in moving away from a representative framework that recognized identities that were regarded as stable and fixed, and towards a model of citizenship centred on the political participation of individuals. Such a model would allow the categories of majority and minority to be constantly defined and redefined within the fluid domain of politics and it would thereby offer the greatest form of security to all citizens.[4]

The key intellectual division among the Constitution-makers was not between those who wanted a united territorial India and those who did not; that issue was settled by Partition, which occurred soon after the Assembly began its work. The key debate in the Constituent Assembly was between those who wanted to assert a conception of individual citizenship in India that went beyond immutable identities (like religion or caste) and those who insisted on Indian nationhood being defined as a confederation of such inescapable identities. Many nationalists who argued passionately outside the Constituent Assembly for a united India (including, many would argue, both Maulana Azad

---

[4] Vallabhbhai Patel, *The Collected Works of Sardar Vallabhbhai Patel*, Vol. I, New Delhi: Konark Publishers, 1990.

and Mahatma Gandhi), nonetheless thought that India was indeed a collection of distinct communities, who could flourish together in amicable coexistence. But the Constituent Assembly, led by Nehru and Ambedkar, went in the opposite direction, consciously opting for individual citizenship as the root of nationhood, transcending the limitations that India's communities imposed on their members.

Ambedkar made this clear. 'I do not believe there is any place in this country for any particular culture, whether it is a Hindu culture, or a Muhammadan culture or a Kanarese culture or a Gujarati culture. There are things we cannot deny, but they are not to be cultivated as advantages, they are to be treated as disadvantages, as something which divides our loyalty and takes away from us our common goal,' he argued. 'That common goal is *the building up of the feeling that we are all Indians*. I do not like what some people say, that we are Indians first and Hindus afterwards or Muslims afterwards. I am not satisfied with that... I do not want that our loyalty as Indians should be in the slightest way affected by any competitive loyalty, whether that loyalty arises out of our religion, out of our culture or out of our language.' (He concluded with the statement I have already quoted, 'I want all people to be Indians first, Indians last and *nothing else but Indians*....')[5]

This fundamental difference of opinion—whether people are Hindus or Muslims first, or Indians first—continues to haunt our politics today. The nationalist movement was divided between two sets of ideas, one held by those who saw religious identity as the determinant of their nationhood, and the other by those who believed in an

---

[5] Quoted in Habib (ed.), *Indian Nationalism*, p. 27. Emphasis added.

inclusive India for everyone, irrespective of faith, where rights were guaranteed to individuals rather than to religious communities. The former became the idea of Pakistan, the latter the idea of India. Pakistan was created as a state with a dominant religion, a state that discriminates against its minorities and denies them equal rights. But India never accepted the logic that had partitioned the country: India's nationalists rejected the argument that just because Pakistan had been created as a homeland for the subcontinent's Muslims, it followed that India should be turned into a Hindu rashtra, the preserve only of the majority community. Our far-seeing founders came down firmly in support of the idea that being Indian had nothing to do with religion, but everything to do with *considering* oneself Indian by virtue of birth and upbringing and belonging. And whoever considered themselves Indians, they affirmed, were entitled to equal rights and privileges.

Article 1 of our Constitution proclaims India to be a Union of States—and nowhere, our Founding Fathers seemed to say, in this union is there space for an exclusionary, extremist, and ethnonationalist state. Thus, they created a pluralist, multi-party democracy where religion was *not* the determinant of nationhood and citizenship and all Indians were free to do their own bidding and dream their own dreams. For these dreams they often strove together, as comrades in a common cause, and when they succeeded, India triumphed. They averred that our freedom struggle was for all, and the newly independent India would also be for all. After the country gained its freedom, the view that was relegated to the fringes throughout the nationalist struggle, and the first four decades of Independence, began to grow in strength and popular appeal in the last four decades—the notion of India as a state identified with the religion professed by the majority—a Hindu rashtra. We will return to this issue shortly.

Constitutions are (and Ambedkar explicitly made this point) tools to control and restrain state power. The challenge lies in reconciling restrictions on state power with popular rule—to prevent temporary majorities (since in a democracy, a majority is temporary, though some people forget that) from completely undoing what the Constitution has provided. In 1975, the union government invoked a constitutional provision to declare an 'internal Emergency' that essentially suspended all the freedoms guaranteed in the Constitution. It arrested critics, censored the press, and made even habeas corpus unenforceable. Its actions were constitutional (since it adhered to the provisions of Article 352 as it existed at the time) but undemocratic. The provision that allowed the declaration of Emergency on the grounds of 'internal disturbances' was significantly amended by the Forty-fourth amendment in 1978 to restrict its misuse by limiting it to 'armed rebellion'. Still, the Emergency of 1975–77 serves as a stark reminder of how far majority rule, if unchecked, can go in the abuse of state power. Khosla suggests that the founders of the Indian republic held a conception of democracy that went beyond majority rule and rejected, in the American legal philosopher Ronald Dworkin's notable phrase, 'the majoritarian premise'.[6] They subordinated politics to law. As Ambedkar put it, the rights of Indian citizens could not 'be taken away by any legislature merely because

---

[6] Ronald Dworkin, *Freedom's Law: The Moral Reading of the American Constitution*, Cambridge: Harvard University Press, 1997, pp. 1–38.

it happens to have a majority'. The Emergency tested this conviction; its end restored it to the heart of India's constitutional democracy.

The struggle for Indian Independence was after all not simply a struggle for freedom from alien rule. It was a shift away from an administration of law and order centred on imperial despotism and colonial subjugation. It was an all-out revolt, symbolized by Gandhian civil disobedience and non-cooperation, against the tyrannical administration of the state. Thus was born the idea of 'constitutional morality', Khosla explains, meaning 'the commitment to constitutional means, to its processes and structures, alongside a commitment to free speech, scrutiny of public action [and] legal limitations on the exercise of power'.[7] This was how freedom was intended to flourish in India. Of course, Ambedkar realized it is perfectly possible to pervert the Constitution, without changing its form, by merely changing the form of the administration to make it inconsistent and opposed to the spirit of the Constitution. Ambedkar argued that constitutional morality 'is not a natural sentiment. It has to be cultivated. We must realize that our people have yet to learn it. Democracy in India is only a top dressing on an Indian soil which is essentially undemocratic'[8]. He insisted that the directive principles—an unusual feature of the Indian Constitution borrowed from the Irish—were necessary because although the rules of democracy mandated that the people must elect those who will hold power, the principles confirmed

---

[7] Khosla, *India's Founding Moment*, p. 42.
[8] From Dr B. R. Ambedkar's speech introducing the Draft Constitution in the Constituent Assembly on 4 November 1948.

that 'whoever captures power will not be free to do what he likes with it'[9].

It is sometimes said that Ambedkar publicly disowned his own Constitution. This makes too much of an emotional speech in Parliament in 1953, when in a testy exchange with other MPs in the Rajya Sabha, he declared: 'We lawyers defend many things. People always keep on saying to me, "Oh! you are the maker of the Constitution." My answer is I was a hack. What I was asked to do, I did much against my will.'[10] The fact is that in the last years of his life Ambedkar was troubled about the majoritarianism inherent in the Constitution. 'It was clear,' he had said before becoming chairman of the Drafting Committee, 'that if the British system was copied it would result in permanently vesting executive power in a communal majority.'[11] As a member of the Constituent Assembly, he went along with its majority view, but in a 1953 interview to the *BBC*, he reiterated in more negative terms something he had already warned against in that Assembly: 'Democracy will not work,' he declared gloomily, 'for the simple reason we have got a social structure which is totally incompatible with parliamentary democracy.'[12]

---

[9] Ibid.
[10] Quoted in Bhanu Dhamija, 'Why Ambedkar Didn't Like India's Constitution', *The Quint*, 14 April 2018. Despite this self-disparagement, Ambedkar's stature has grown enormously since his passing; in his lifetime he lost almost every election he contested, including two runs for the Lok Sabha, but today he is arguably amongst the most revered of Indians, his birthday the occasion of a five-night vigil by his devoted followers, his statues across the country second only in number to those of Mahatma Gandhi. See Shashi Tharoor, *Ambedkar: A Life*, New Delhi: Aleph Book Company, 2022.
[11] Ibid.
[12] Ibid.

In the Constitution, Ambedkar, despite these public and private misgivings, took a more optimistic view of the prospects of democracy in India by asking Indians to have a new understanding of authority. They would be liberated through submission to an impersonal force that saw them as equal agents, and that liberated spirit would make possible socio-economic transformation. Both were equally important. Both Nehru and Ambedkar understood that India's Constitution had to meet the need for three things simultaneously: strength, to resist external aggression, discipline, to resist internal fissures, and 'scientific advancement', to promote economic justice and stability. At the same time the founders of the Indian republic worried about democracy becoming an elections-only affair, and of a popular mandate degenerating into majoritarianism. In the Constituent Assembly, the prime minister and home minister of the time, Jawaharlal Nehru and Sardar Patel, went to great lengths to limit their own power—a thought simply unimaginable today.

To the Constitution-makers, India's Independence Day was not meant to be just a ritual of song and dance, the hoisting of the flag, and the singing of the national anthem. The real significance of Independence lay in the freedom of the mind. Indians were meant to be able to recognize and overcome, in Tagore's immortal phrase, a world that had 'been broken up into fragments by narrow domestic walls'.[13] The multifaceted philosopher and thinker explained further, 'My countrymen will gain truly their India by fighting against that education which teaches them that a country

---

[13] Rabindranath Tagore, *Gitanjali: Song Offerings* (1912), Keighley: Pomona Press, 2007.

is greater than the ideals of humanity.'[14]

This was an unusual kind of nationalist idea. But it led to the second overriding objective, less Tagore's than that of leaders like Jawaharlal Nehru—that democracy in India would need to necessarily entail equality and a decent standard of living for all. For Nehru, the establishment of a free and democratic India required the substitution of the economic power of a few rich individuals by a form of state control that could end poverty, reduce unemployment, and improve material conditions. After all, the egregious Winston Churchill had predicted that after the departure of the British, 'India will fall back quite rapidly through the centuries into the barbarism and privations of the Middle Ages.'[15] Nehru knew that Independence would be justified only by giving the lie to such prophecies through development and progress.

The Indian Constitution had a centralized bent, despite Mahatma Gandhi's long advocacy of constitutional arrangements being built from the ground up, starting with self-sustaining village republics at the bottom of the pyramid. Gandhi had rejected the idea of imitating the British parliamentary system, seeking instead a system more suited to what he described as the Indian genius: 'I have described it as Ram Rajya—sovereignty of the people based on pure moral authority.' Neither Ambedkar nor Nehru were sympathizers of this point of view. Ambedkar was particularly sarcastic about support for the Gandhian idea amongst some members of the Constituent Assembly: 'The

---

[14] Rabindranath Tagore, *Nationalism*, London: Macmillan and Co., Ltd, 1918.
[15] Ramachandra Guha, 'An Unlikely Nation', *New Statesman*, 2 August 2007.

love of the intellectual Indians for the village community,' he sardonically observed, 'is of course infinite if not pathetic.' Ambedkar was scathing about the prejudices and casteism rife in Indian villages: 'What is the village but a sink of localism, a den of ignorance, narrow-mindedness, and communalism? I am glad that the draft Constitution has discarded the village.'

The liberal institutions of our Constitution give every member of our polity an opportunity to pursue their constitutional rights. The Congress-led UPA government (2004–14) ensured the rearming of India's rights regime (with the Right to Information Act, the Mahatma Gandhi National Rural Employment Guarantee Scheme, the Right to Education Act, and other liberal entitlements such as to food security and welfare), along with near double digit economic growth, a dramatic drop in the number of Indians living below the poverty line, and even a nuclear deal with the US. It is that form of democracy, informed by Nehru's vision, and undergirded by civic nationalism, which built an entire edifice of rights for Indians, that is under challenge from today's hyper-nationalist forces.

The Constitution of India established the shared norms on which self-government rests, in particular the statutory equality of every citizen, irrespective of religion, region, or language. India's civic nationalism is both created by and reflected in its provisions. The governments it commands are supposed to be committed to the welfare of the country's weakest citizens. Though poverty, social discrimination, and caste tyranny still persist, the Constitution offers the victims protection and redress. Amid the myriad problems of India, it is constitutional democracy that has given Indians of every imaginable caste, creed, culture, and cause the chance to break free of their lot and fulfil their aspirations. This possibility rests on a core assumption of civic nationalism: the development and strengthening of free institutions that ensure pluralism, protect diversity, and guarantee the integrity of the state.

V

A Living Document

As we have seen in the preceding chapter, the Constitution established for the first time the notion of individual rights as the basis for Indians' participation in their democratic polity.

At the same time, the Constitution acknowledged group rights, such as the right of religious denominations to establish and maintain institutions for religious and charitable purposes (Article 26(a)), or the right of a 'section of the citizens' to conserve a distinct language, script, or culture (Article 29(1)). There was a lively debate on the issue of a national language, with advocates of Hindi facing staunch opposition from non-Hindi-speaking states, mainly in the South and the East, who argued for India's diversity and the preservation of English as a link language. There were also provisions to ensure affirmative action for Scheduled Castes, to protect the interests of Scheduled Tribes (Articles 15(4) and 19(5)) and the specific language of Articles 25 and 26, casting an implicit heavy responsibility on the majority to ensure that minorities feel secure. But though the Constitution thus recognized groups as bearing constitutional rights—thus departing from the 'singular unification' model—former chief justice Dhananjaya Y. Chandrachud of the Supreme Court has argued that this 'was nested in the understanding that membership of groups had a unique role of crafting and determining individual identity.... In elevating groups as distinct rights holders as well as empowering state intervention to address historical injustice and inequality perpetrated by group membership, the framers located liberalism within the pluralist reality of India and conceptualized every individual as located at an intersection between liberal individualism and plural belonging.... At the time of its birth, the nation was conceptualized as incorporating its vast diversity and not eliminating it.'[1]

This ability to recognize groups and yet adjudicate the rights of their individual members, and the adaptability of the Constitution to the ever-changing realities of national life, have effectively made it a vehicle of social change. 'The Constitution is not an ephemeral legal document embodying a set of legal rules for the passing hour', the Supreme Court itself observed in its judgement in M. *Nagaraj & Ors. vs Union of India & Ors.* 'It sets out principles for an expanding future and is intended to endure for ages to come and consequently to be adapted to the various crises of human affairs.' Equally important, this process has been substantially facilitated by our Parliament. The Constitution created itself as a self generating and self-correcting entity, a living document that allowed for its own amendment to meet the changes of the times. Dr Ambedkar pointed out that he had no intention of 'putting a seal of finality and infallibility upon this Constitution'.

The Founding Fathers knew that with changing circumstances, the aspirations of Indians, and the ways in

---

[1] Dhananjaya Y. Chandrachud, 'The Hues That Are India: From Plurality to Pluralism', Justice P. D. Desai Memorial Lecture 2020, 15 February 2020, Gujarat High Court.

which they can be realized, would evolve; so they drafted a 'transformative Constitution', to borrow a phrase from the legal scholar Gautam Bhatia,[2] which they equipped for all time to come with the tools that would allow us to 'wipe every tear from every eye', as Gandhi wanted us to. The Constitution has therefore been amended over a hundred times by Parliament, an institution created inter alia for that very purpose by the Constitution. (The American Constitution has been amended only twenty-seven times since 1789.) The small-minded may consider the high number of amendments as one of the weaknesses of our Constitution, but those with a broader vision would understand that it is actually a sign of its inherent strength—a strength that derives from its ability to be flexible without the risk of self-destruction. It has the exemplary in-built ability to adjust to the needs of the times and the fact that this is enabled through a thoroughly democratic and representative process has been key to its effectiveness in moving our society forward in a more broadly inclusive manner.

During the journey of the Constitution, there have been innumerable instances which have either corroded or nurtured this central idea. Great progress took place under the purview of Jawaharlal Nehru. The First Amendment in 1951 abolished zamindari or feudal landlordism (though this went against the right to property), and placed 'reasonable' restrictions on free speech, much to the dismay of libertarians, while the Seventh Amendment in 1956 laid the foundation for the establishment of states on linguistic lines. The creation of states, union territories, and their autonomy, brought many

---

[2] Gautam Bhatia, 'Citizenship and the Constitution', Yale University Law School paper, 31 March 2020.

of the Northeastern states and new territories to the Indian union, and provided legitimacy to extending the embrace of India to these territories. But it also asserted the primacy of the union, the centre: India was not, unlike the US, a collection of states coming together to constitute a nation, but a long-standing nation through the ages that had the power to create states as sub-units of itself.

During the Emergency, the Forty-second Amendment in 1976, involving various articles, brought two key principles of the Indian idea, hitherto implicit rather than explicit, formally into the Preamble of the Constitution—'Socialist and Secular'. The idea of India is inseparable from these ideas, the dark period of their insertion notwithstanding, which is why no subsequent government has undone them so far, even if the original Constitution-makers had considered it unnecessary to insert these words into the document when the Preamble was adopted in 1949. A 2020 petition seeking for the words to be removed was rejected in 2024 by the Supreme Court, whose judges observed that both terms reflect the actual spirit of the Constitution, even if the words themselves were inserted later. (More on this debate later.)

Various other amendments to the Constitution (the Twenty-third, Forty-fifth, Fifty-first amendments, among others) have tried to make the basic nature of India more inclusive as they tried to protect the interests of vulnerable sections of Indian society. Activist judges have taken the Constitution beyond strict legislation to promote human rights and welfare in a series of landmark judgements. As one of the world's largest democracies, India has struggled to provide education to all its children; the landmark Eighty-sixth Amendment was passed as the Right to Education

Act in 2009 conferring on all children in the age group of six to fourteen years the right to free and compulsory education. The Right to Information Act, passed in June 2005, which shored up the participatory nature of our democracy, empowering the citizenry and making public officials more accountable, is another hallmark of how the law guides and derives value from the principles of civic nationalism and of governmental subordination to the Indian people. By ensuring the disclosure of information on demand to the Indian public, the law enshrined in the Constitution of our land emphatically acknowledges their right to accountability. The Right to Life under Article 21 was interpreted to include the 'Right to Know'. The 2017 Puttaswamy judgement affirming the Right to Privacy has bolstered this indispensable element of the citizen's freedom. This framework of rights—to knowledge, information, education, and privacy—have asserted a new infrastructure of empowered citizenship that is indispensable in a participatory democracy. The Constitution incorporates the understanding that if India is truly to flourish, equality must not only be political—it must also be economic and social, and extend its protective socio-economic cover to lakhs of citizens who have woefully resided on the margins of our national consciousness.

But this power of amendment is subject to the Doctrine of Basic Structure, again an invention of the judiciary. Two quotes from Supreme Court judgements trace the remarkable evolution of this doctrine. In *I. C. Golaknath & Ors. vs State of Punjab, 1967*, it observed:

> We have given careful consideration to the argument that certain basic features of our Constitution cannot

be amended under article 368 and have come to the conclusion that no limitations can be and should be implied upon the power of amendment under Article 368. One reason for coming to this conclusion is that if we were to accept that certain basic features of the Constitution cannot be amended under Article 368, it will lead to the position that any amendment made to any Article of the Constitution would be liable to challenge before courts on the ground that it amounts to amendment of a basic feature.

But six years later, the Supreme Court of India changed its mind and decided there was indeed a Basic Structure to the Constitution that could not be amended. In *Kesavananda Bharati Sripadagalvaru & Ors. vs State of Kerala, 1973*, it declared:

> When we speak of the 'abrogation' or 'repeal' of the Constitution, we do not refer to any form but to substance. If one or more of the basic features of the Constitution are taken away, to that extent the Constitution is abrogated or repealed. If all the basic features of the Constitution are repealed and some other provisions inconsistent with those features are incorporated, it cannot still remain the Constitution referred to in Article 368. The personality of the Constitution must remain unchanged.

The Basic Structure Doctrine may be firmly established, but its contents are yet to be fully defined or conclusively settled. In *L. Chandra Kumar, 1997*, the Supreme Court ruled that judicial review forms a part of this basic structure while in *Kihoto Hollohan vs Zachillhu, 1992*, it unanimously recognized democracy as a key feature of this doctrine. This includes free and fair elections based on universal adult franchise and the multiparty system. Notably, secularism has also been recognized as a basic feature in *S. R. Bommai vs Union of India, 1994*, along with federalism. Among other features, the Supreme Court has included the rule of law (*S. P. Sampath Kumar vs Union of India, 1987*), the independence of the judiciary (*Kumar Padma Prasad vs Union of India, 1992*) and equality (*Indra Sawhney vs Union of India, 2000*). Furthermore, the very unamendability of the basic structure also constitutes a part of the basic structure (*Minerva Mills Ltd. vs Union of India, 1980*). What's most striking is that only the judiciary interprets and determines the scope of this doctrine. There is every possibility that future cases could identify additional elements that are deemed to be parts of the Basic Structure and thus beyond legislative amendment.

VI

Moving Beyond the Provisions

In the recent past, the Anna Hazare movement[1], a popular agitation in the main cities of India in 2011–14 that clamoured for legislation to install an all-powerful national ombudsman, raised the question of the role of civil society in determining legislative priorities in our democracy. A Lokpal Bill was introduced by the government in Parliament in response to the strength of numbers in the streets. Members of Parliament felt they had no choice but to go along with this, though some who had serious misgivings about the bill privately wondered what their role was supposed to be, with Parliament's law-making functions being encroached upon by civil society on the one hand and the judiciary (through its innovative but intrusive 'Public Interest Litigations') on the other.

There is no doubt that today's lawmakers face new and tougher challenges than ever before. The rapid advancement and penetration of information technology, improving social indicators, the change in demography, the growing economic prowess of our nation, the rise of new global threats, and our ever-greater international integration, all impose new

---

[1] R. Chowdhury, S. Banerjee, D. S. Nagarkoti, 'Anna Hazare: A Corruption Crusader and His Grassroots Wisdom', *Journal of Management Inquiry*, Volume 26, Issue 4, 2017, pp. 383–89; Soutik Biswas, 'Anna Hazare's movement - a reality check for India', *BBC*, 28 August 2011.

constraints on the sovereign function of law-making, even as they also allow new opportunities. The techniques for surveillance being developed by the government—and whose use received a boost with the imperative need to track those who might have been exposed to carriers of the coronavirus in 2020—could, in a post-Covid-19 world, be used to trace the movements and contacts of citizens, the Right to Privacy notwithstanding.

The civil society protests of a decade ago add another challenge. In a democracy, there are specific rights accorded to citizens by the state to help them exercise their political freedoms: freedom of speech and political association and related rights allow citizens—in other words, members of civil society—to get together, argue and discuss, debate and criticize, protest and strike (and in Kerala—mainly in Kerala!—to declare hartals inconveniencing the general public), and even go on fasts and hunger strikes, in order to support or challenge their governments. This is an essential part of promoting governmental accountability between elections: no one can seriously argue that a citizen's democratic rights begin and end with the right to choose his government through voting alone. Indeed, as the Nobel-prize winning economist Amartya Sen so brilliantly asserted with reference to India in his *The Argumentative Indian: Writings on Indian Culture, History and Identity*, it is through perpetual discussions and engagement with 'the reach of reason' that a deliberative democracy is created.[2]

Sen's emphasis on robust discourse in India is derided by his critics as upper caste, male, classist, academic. After

---

[2] Amartya Sen, *The Argumentative Indian: Writings on Indian History, Culture and Identity*, New York: Farrar, Straus and Giroux, 2006, p. 273.

all, they ask, who gets to speak in India, to whom, and how? Speech is deeply imbued with class, caste, gender, and educational bias. This is hardly unique to India: the US did not reserve a place at the high table for Africans, Native Americans, the Irish, and the Chinese at various times, and the Dred Scott decision in 1857 even declared that free blacks, as the descendants of slaves, were not citizens. As opposed to that, India had a constitutionally based, far-reaching affirmative action programme for its Dalits at a time when many US states were still denying large numbers of blacks the vote. Democracy takes time to evolve and deepen; its imperfections are not cause to dismiss it, but rather to affirm the vital importance of improving and strengthening it.

In any discussion of a Constitution, there is often a useful distinction to be made between law and legitimacy: law is passed by legislatures at the behest of the executive under the Constitution, but legitimacy inheres in the representative character of those proposing and enacting the law, and in the extent to which they are seen as embodying, and acting upon, the best interests of the people as a whole. The greater the extent to which ordinary people are engaged with, concerned by, and empowered to determine their own political destiny, the more they accept the decisions of the state institutions, and the more legitimate the law becomes to the people. One is reminded of the famous formulation of Rousseau:

> It is to law alone that men owe justice and liberty. It is this salutary organ of the will of all which establishes in civil rights the natural equality between men. It is this celestial voice which dictates to each citizen the precepts of public reason, and teaches him to act

according to the rules of his own judgment and not to behave inconsistently with himself. It is with this voice alone that political leaders should speak when they command.[3]

So, to that extent, civil society does and should have an influence on law-making. But that is not the same thing as saying it should have a direct role. In Switzerland, for example, ordinary citizens can actually bypass the elected legislature and write laws by proposing and then voting for these propositions in referenda that are organized by the state and whose outcomes are recognized by the government as having the full binding force of law. That is not the case, however, in most other democracies, where civil society's impact is confined to the influence it is able to bring to bear on the elected lawmakers, through the shaping of public opinion, effective lobbying, media campaigns, and mass movements.

In India, under our Constitution, we preserve the national idea by enabling these key aspects of the democratic process. This could be said to suit the democratic temper of our people. In ancient times, our civilization had sabhas and samitis where kingdoms and even empires were ruled on the principle of democratic functioning, extending right from the grass-roots level in the form of panchayats and councils, which represented the broad as well as specific segments of the populace, to the royal courts where maharajas took advice from learned and wise elders. This tradition is important to recall, since it confirms that both majority as well as minority

---

[3] Jean-Jacques Rousseau, *The Social Contract,* translated by Maurice Cranston, London: Penguin Books, 2001.

opinion were given due importance in the formulation of public policy. This was no mean achievement in a nation and society as diverse and heterogeneous as India, with its innumerable groups and socio-religious identities. The law has the responsibility to preserve this diversity, allow each individual component to feel secure within it, and yet guide the nation's progressive evolution.

Under the Constitution of India, Parliament is the supreme legislative body at the national level. Only Parliament makes laws that affect the entire country and therefore help shape its society. The most important aspect of legislation lies in its vital social or sociological ramifications—think, for example, of the reservations policy for certain castes, decided by Parliament, which has proved a remarkable tool of social mobility and political transformation. Parliament has also not been found wanting in creating through legislation many institutions and mechanisms which today address issues crucial to the well-being of our society.

The process of democratic elections in India, involving a multiplicity of political parties organized to reflect any conceivable interest and ideology in society, ensures the representative character of Parliament—and this in turn is reflected in the manner in which its members perform their legislative functions. This is why laws must be made by lawmakers who, being elected by the people, are truly representative of the society they are seeking to regulate, and who are bound by oath to act for the fair and equal welfare of all sections of the people they are constitutionally elected to represent.

This healthy spirit of recognition and acceptance of difference, of constitutional encouragement of debate and discussion, fuelled by a thriving free media, vocal civil society forums, energetic human rights groups, assorted autonomous institutions, and the repeated spectacle of our remarkable general elections, are all assets for India's civic nationalism. Together with a fractious and competitive political culture, sustained by the protective framework of the Constitution, they have made India a rare example of the successful management of diversity in the developing world.

VII

An Alternative Idea of India

The idea of India I have described, embodied in the Constitution, is that of civic nationalism sanctified by Indic civilization and suffused by an ethos of pluralism. This was the Indian nationalists' answer to the challenge posed by Partition. On the other hand, the alternative was the Hindutva idea of a Hindu country, espoused today by the Sangh Parivar led by the BJP and the RSS, the mirror image of the idea of Pakistan—a state with a dominant majority religion that seeks to put its minorities in a subordinate place. Its ethnic (religious, cultural, and linguistic) nationalism is often summarized in the slogan 'Hindi–Hindu[tva]–Hindustan'. This is the principal alternative to the civic nationalist conception of India.

At the time of the Constitution's adoption, only one strain of politics rejected it—the Hindu nationalist elements organized under the Hindu Mahasabha, the Rashtriya Swayamsevak Sangh (RSS), and its political offshoot the Bharatiya Jana Sangh (which later morphed into today's Bharatiya Janata Party, BJP).[1] The two-nation theory, that revolting idea which metamorphosed into Pakistan, was not endorsed by

---

[1] Shamsul Islam, '68th anniversary of Indian constitution: when nation celebrated its adoption, RSS mourned it', *National Herald*, 27 November 2017, Subhashini Ali, 'Thirty Years After the Demolition', 7 March 2023, *Marxist*, XXXVIII, 4, Oct–Dec 2022.

the Muslim League alone; the Hindu Mahasabha and the RSS had also argued that Hindus and Muslims were two distinct nations with irreconcilable historical, religious, and cultural differences, making their coexistence in a united India impossible.[2] These arguments were reaffirmed by both Vinayak Damodar Savarkar, the father of Hindu nationalism, in his *Essentials of Hindutva* in 1923, and by M. S. Golwalkar in *We or Our Nationhood Defined* in 1939, a year before he became the sarsanghchalak or supremo of the RSS. When the Constitution was adopted, they, and their associates, argued that India had written—in the wrong language!—a Constitution imitative of the West, based on alien Western ideas of nationhood, and divorced from any real connection to the Hindu mode of life and from authentically Indian ideas about the relationship between the individual and society.[3]

The Jan Sangh ideologue Deen Dayal Upadhyaya, who articulated this view most cogently, was echoing Golwalkar, who had lamented that our 'cumbersome' Constitution was all the more deficient for incorporating 'absolutely nothing' from the Manusmriti—also known as the Laws of Manu or Manava-Dharmashastra—the ancient Hindu legal and ethical text, attributed to the sage Manu and believed to have been compiled between the second century BCE and the third century CE. The Manusmriti provides guidance on various aspects of life, including social organization, duties, and responsibilities of individuals, marriage, inheritance, and punishments for offences, and is hailed by the Sangh

---

[2] 'Hindu Mahasabha was first to give two-nation theory: Cong spokesperson Khera', *Business Standard*, 29 June 2019.
[3] Karan Thapar, 'Full Text | Constitution, Majority, BJP: What an RSS Chief Told Karan Thapar Decades Ago', *The Wire*, 17 December 2024.

Parivar as India's foundational legal charter.[4] But while, over the years, the Manusmriti has had a profound impact on Hindu law and society, it is fiercely contested because it specifies duties, behaviours, and restrictions for different castes and genders, in a manner that demeans the so-called 'lower' castes and women. (Ambedkar, who ceremonially burned a copy of the Manusmriti in 1927, would scarcely have been willing to take it into account in drafting the Constitution two decades later.)

Upadhyaya felt the need for a Constitution reflecting a Hindu political philosophy befitting an ancient nation like Bharat. This would, he argued, have to be based on a 'positive concept of patriotism' and a comprehensive vision of the nation as a complete entity—its security, its unity, its growth and development, the welfare of its entire populace and the full development of every individual—based on its inherent character, culture, spiritual underpinnings, and enduring values. By granting equal citizenship and equal rights to Muslims and other non-Hindus, said Upadhyaya, the Constitution had erred, for Indian nationalism had to be Hindu nationalism. Like Savarkar and Golwalkar before him, Upadhyaya deplored the concept of territorial nationalism embodied in the Constitution, which saw the Indian nation as being formed of all the peoples who reside in this land. Upadhyaya was clear, like Savarkar and Golwalkar, that the Constitution was wrong to reduce the Indian national idea and its people to a territory. (The rejection of 'territorial nationalism' is fundamental to all the principal thinkers of

---

[4] M. P. Raju, 'Composite culture and its discontents', *Frontline*, 17 August 2017; Jawhar Sircar, 'Constitution vs Manusmriti: The Sangh owes it to India to clarify its position', *Scroll.in*, 26 January 2025.

the Hindutva project.) Rather than the constitutional idea of India as a territory inhabited by people of different faiths and united by the 'negative patriotism' of anti-colonialism, Upadhyaya argued, the key ingredient of true nationalism was love for the motherland, 'a sense of "my-ness".'[5] India could and should contribute to the world 'in consonance with our culture and traditions'. That culture and those traditions were, of course, Hindu, and embodied in texts like the Manusmriti. In India, 'there exists only one culture.... There are no separate cultures here for Muslims and Christians'.

Upadhyaya's argument was that the Muslims sought 'to destroy the values of Indian culture, its ideals, national heroes, traditions, places of devotion and worship', and therefore 'can never become an indivisible part of this country'. In Upadhyaya's vision, the inherent consciousness of unity, identical ties of history and tradition, relations of affinity between the land and the people and shared aspirations and hopes, made Hindustan a nation of Hindus. 'We shall have to concede that our nationality is none other than Hindu nationality. If any outsider comes into this country he shall have to move in step and adjust himself with Hindu nationality.'

In building a case for his formulation, Upadhyaya specifically disavowed the Constitution of India (which makes all the more curious the enthusiastic zeal with which his devotees today, from Prime Minister Modi on down, swear by it and celebrate every milestone in its adoption).

---

[5] The quotes from and relating to Upadhyaya's views may be found in K. S. Bharathi, *The Political Thought of Pandit Deendayal Upadhyaya*, New Delhi: Concept Publishing Company, 1998, p. 86; C. P. Bhishkar, *Pt. Deendayal Upadhyay: Ideology & Perception–Part 5: Concept of The Rashtra*, New Delhi: Suruchi Prakashan, 2014, p. 4; and V. V. Nene, *Pandit Deendayal Upadhyaya: Ideology and Perception*, translated by M. K. Paranjape and D. R. Kulkarni, New Delhi: Suruchi Prakashan, 1988.

As Upadhyaya put it in *Rashtra Jeevan Ki Disha*: 'Indian leaders...failed to see that our inherent national ideals and traditions should be reflected in our Constitution.... The result was that our national culture and traditions were never reflected in these ideologies borrowed from elsewhere and so they utterly failed to touch the chords of our national being.'[6] The Constitution's core conception of the nation, in his view, was fundamentally not Indian at all. 'In the Constitution, as it is now, it is the sentiments of the English that have found better expression than those of the Indians,' observed Upadhyaya. Having rejected its premise, Upadhyaya was scathing about the Constitution's drafting and adoption: a nation, he argued, 'is not like a club which can be started or dissolved. A nation is not created by some crores of people passing a resolution and defining a common code of behaviour binding on all its members. A certain mass of people emerges with an inherent motivation. It is,' he added, using a Hindu analogy, 'like the soul adopting the medium of the body.'

Upadhyaya (and the strain of thought embodied in what is today called the Sangh Parivar) thus questioned the very legitimacy of the Constitution—and not just of the process by which it was created or the language in which it was written. For Upadhyaya, the absence of the 'Hindu rashtra' idea in the Constitution was unacceptable. For him dharma had to be the central idea behind governance and nation building. In keeping with his distaste for foreign concepts and terms, Upadhyaya explicated his beliefs through the use of Sanskrit terms to which he ascribed specific contemporary meanings. A favourite word of Upadhyaya's is chiti, which

---

[6] Upadhyaya, *Rashtra Jeevan Ki Disha*.

he labels the 'soul power' of a nation. He describes this soul power through a homely analogy: a barber told his customer that his razor was sixty years old, and had been used by his father. Upon further scrutiny, the customer noticed that over the years the handle and blade had been replaced many times, but the barber still claimed that the razor was the same as used by his father. It was a point of pride and prestige for him: the essence of the razor was unchanged even if its physical trappings had been altered over the years. Every nation also had such an identity that did not change with circumstances and temporal alterations. Sadly, modern India—the democratic republic that had emerged under the Constitution—had no sense of its chiti.

One example of this was in the country's constitutional structure. Upadhyaya saw the seeds of division, for instance, even in the Constitution's decision to rename the provinces as 'states' as the Americans did; this reduced India to a federation of states, a dangerously divisive concept in his view. Upadhyaya acknowledged that, unlike the US, every Indian state did not have its own Constitution and that there was only one citizenship for the entire country, but he felt the formulation envisaged in the Constitution diluted the sacred idea of a unified Bharatvarsha. The Constitution should have spoken of a unitary state rather than a union of states; the chiti of Bharat was missing. He seemed unconscious of the argument that it was precisely because of these states and their linguistic basis that unity was achieved, for India was able to accommodate all its diversities and give them political expression without losing the bigger cause of united nationhood. But to him the diversity guaranteed by the Constitution was not a positive. A unitary nation imbued with the spirit of chiti creates virat shakti, the organized and unified fighting strength that protects the nation from aggression and dissension. While chiti is the soul of a nation, virat shakti is its life force. Of course, neither idea is even implicitly present in India's Constitution, underscoring, for Upadhyaya, its deeply flawed nature.

The critics of 'Hindu rashtra', Upadhyaya argued, found that the term was inexpedient for them in the country's competitive politics: they were afraid of losing millions of Christian and Muslim voters. Their misconception was that the use of the term 'Hindu rashtra' excluded Muslim and Christian communities. If both these communities became one with the national cultural mainstream—without any change in their modes of worship—they would be welcome in the new India. All they had to do was to own up to the ancient traditions of India, to look upon Hindu national heroes as their national heroes, and to develop devotion for Bharat Mata. Then they would be fully accepted as nationals of the Hindu India that he envisioned. But the Constitution that granted them this acceptance could not be the one adopted in English by Anglophone elites imbued with Western ideas. A truly Indian—that is to say, Hindu—document would have to be written.

VIII

A Challenge to the Constitution: Whither Secularism and Pluralism?

As we have seen, and as Gautam Bhatia has well described, the Constitution articulates 'a vision of Indian citizenship that is interwoven with Indian constitutional identity as a whole: secular, egalitarian, and non-discriminatory. Drawing upon universal humanist principles—and in specific and conscious contrast to the State of Pakistan—the Constituent Assembly crafted an idea of citizenship that rejected markers of identity, whether ethnic or religious'.[1] As Partition refugees streamed across the border in the largest exodus then known to humanity, fleeing religious violence, Alladi Krishnaswamy Ayyar, a veteran lawyer, advised the Assembly that, 'It is for you to consider whether our conception of citizenship should be universal, or should be racial or should be sectarian.'[2] The Constituent Assembly specifically debated whether it should recognize nationality (in an ethnic sense) or citizenship (in a non-racial, 'universal' sense) before opting for the latter. As K. M. Munshi observed: 'The world is divided between the ideas of racial citizenship and democratic citizenship, and therefore, the words "born in India" become necessary to indicate that

---

[1] Bhatia, 'Citizenship and the Constitution'.
[2] Ibid.

we align ourselves with the democratic principle.'[3]

Conversely, P. S. Deshmukh spoke for those who wanted an explicitly religious basis for citizenship: he proposed that 'every person who is a Hindu or a Sikh by religion and is not a citizen of any other State, wherever he resides' should be eligible to be Indian. This was rejected after a debate in which Ayyar reminded the Assembly that 'we are plighted to the principles of a secular State'.[4] The Constitution, in other words, linked citizenship very specifically to the idea of a non-communal, non-denominational polity, without distinction of religion, race, caste, or class—the idea of India again. The 'rigorously universal and non-discriminatory language' of the constitutional provisions for citizenship, in Bhatia's words, 'were never intended to be read in isolation. Rather, they formed one strand in a web of harmonious and mutually reinforcing principles, which, woven together, made up the Constitution'. Citizenship was linked to 'a coherent and morally consistent political vision' of Indian nationhood.[5]

This was the constitutional background to the practice of Indian secularism, which took pride in the fact that its citizenship was held by people of all conceivable religions and ethnicities. Foreigners—including former US president George W. Bush—had admired the fact that despite being home to 180 million Muslims, India had produced hardly

---

[3] Speech of K. M. Munshi, Parliament of India, *Constituent Assembly Debates*, Vol. 3, 29 April 1947.
[4] *Constituent Assembly Debates*, Vol. 9, 11 August 1949. For a fascinating summary of the debate, see Aditya Chatterjee, 'How the Constituent Assembly Debated (and Rejected) Citizenship by Religion', *The Wire*, 10 February 2020.
[5] Bhatia, 'Citizenship and the Constitution'.

any members of ISIS or Al-Qaeda.[6] Indians would point with pride to the fact that this was because Indian democracy gave Muslims an equal stake in the country's well-being. Sadly, we can no longer say that now.

The reason for fearing that this stake is now diluted is a recent [late 2019] challenge to, arguably, the most fundamental aspect of Indianness, through a law, the Citizenship (Amendment) Act (CAA), which fast-tracks citizenship for people fleeing persecution in Pakistan, Afghanistan, and Bangladesh—provided they are not Muslim. It is, without question, the first law to question a basic building block of our nation—that religion is not the determinant of our nationhood and, therefore, of our citizenship. The implications of this law immediately created an increase in tensions and a wave of protests around the country, leading to an eruption of violence in the nation's capital that claimed fifty-three lives[7] and left hundreds injured. It has also hurt the perception of India as an inclusive state which honours the equality of all and guarantees that the state will not practice religious discrimination. By excluding members of just one community, the new law is antithetical to India's secular and pluralist traditions.

The implications—constitutional, political, social, and moral—are profound. The Act paves the way not only for declaring immigrants to be illegal if they happen to be Muslim, but coupled with an even more problematic National Register of Citizens the government announced that it intends

---

[6] Chidanand Rajghatta, 'Bush praises Indian democracy', *Times of India*, 7 November 2003.

[7] Joanna Slater, Niha Misah, 'In Delhi's worst violence in decades, a man watched his brother burn', *Washington Post*, 6 March 2020; 'Killed by hate', *Al Jazeera Interactive*.

to create (though it has since been deferred), would allow it to disenfranchise any Indian Muslim who is unable to prove his antecedents. Many Indians, especially the poor, do not have documentary evidence of when and where they were born; even birth certificates have only become widespread in recent decades. While non-Muslims would, thanks to this Act, get a free pass, similarly undocumented Muslims would suddenly face the onus of proving they are Indian.

It is, in many ways, a breathtaking departure from over seven decades of democratic practice in a country that was proud of its impressive record of managing stunning levels of diversity. As we have seen, the Constituent Assembly had rejected separate electorates, weighted representation, and reservations on the basis of religion. Yet the CAA for the first time introduced religion into a citizenship law in India. Our nationalist struggle had split on this question; it was by rejecting the extreme, exclusivist idea of Pakistan that our founders enshrined in the Constitution an all-inclusive, secular idea of India, which fostered a civic nationalism—as against an ethno-nationalism based on religion, language, culture, and ethnicity—ensuring that all those who call this land their home are equal citizens with equal rights, irrespective of all differences. Yet this fundamental question, of whether religion should be the determinant of Indian nationhood and citizenship, continues to haunt our politics. The religious bigotry that partitioned the country with the founding of Pakistan has now been mirrored in pluralist India. As I told my fellow parliamentarians, that was a partition in the Indian soil; this is now a partition of the Indian soul.

The Act's supporters in the BJP were belligerent about their bigotry. 'If Hindus cannot find a home in India, where can they?' was their refrain. Their implicit argument, like that of Savarkar and Upadhyaya, is that India is a natural Hindu homeland; Muslims have other countries they can lay claim to. That was not what India was supposed to be: the shocking thing about this argument is that, in one piece of bigoted legislation, it sweeps aside the fundamental premise of Indian nationalism. The CAA is not just an affront to the basic tenets of equality and religious non-discrimination that have been enshrined in Articles 14 and 15 of our Constitution, but an all-out assault on the basic assumptions of the republic.

The BJP, which prefers to polarize[8] the electorate by consolidating a majority 'Hindu vote' in every election[9], was quick to paint the anti-CAA agitation in communal colours, as Hindu vs Muslim.[10] I urged Muslim protestors not to play into their hands by saying they were protesting as Muslims, which would only facilitate the other side's efforts to divide opinion on communal lines. 'Say instead that you are fighting for your rights as Indian citizens, and every right-thinking Indian will empathize with you,' I argued. India's resistance to injustice embraces all communities. I don't have to be Muslim to object to Muslims being discriminated against in their own country. By creating a republic where all faiths are safe, India's Constitution protects Muslims as well as others. We're all in this together.

The Constitution is clearly under stress. Indian

---

[8] Sharanya Hrishikesh & Vikas Pandey, 'Narendra Modi's India: A decade of popularity and polarisation', *BBC*, 17 May 2024.
[9] See, for example, Anand Mishra, 'BJP falls back on Hindutva after election setbacks', *Frontline*, 7 August 2024.
[10] See '"Shoot the Traitors" Discrimination Against Muslims under India's New Citizenship Policy', Human Rights Watch, 9 April 2020.

nationalism, in precept and practice, had acquired a significantly identifiable character in the decades after the country won freedom but is being pressed to undergo fundamental change today. During the anti-colonial struggle against the British, the nationalist movement had many of the characteristics of classic ethno-cultural nationalism—the Indian people, harking back to their ancient civilization, fought for self-determination against the foreign oppressor. Upon Independence, and with the writing of a secular and liberal democratic Constitution, India's nationalism became a form of civic nationalism, though no political leader specifically used the term. Today, with the ascent of a 'Hindi–Hindu[tva]–Hindustan' sentiment in the ruling circles of the country, India's nationalism is being forced to transform into a combination of religious, linguistic, and cultural nationalism, its liberal–democratic trappings increasingly discarded in the pursuit of a loyal conformity that alone, in the eyes of the dominant establishment, is acceptable as truly nationalist.

Since freedom of speech and association and representative democracy are not totally inconsistent with the majoritarian impulse, those of us wedded to civic nationalism must rely on liberal constitutionalism (and functioning, autonomous, democratic institutions) to resist majoritarianism. We must affirm the principles embedded in the Constitution, if the country is not to descend into an ethno-nationalist 'illiberal democracy'.

The great question before us today is, therefore: will constitutionalism tame Hindutva, or will Hindutva transform the workings of the Constitution from a democracy to a 'dharmocracy'? Can Hindutva change with the times, particularly since its acolytes are now in power, and when the CAA was adopted, for the first time in the history of India, its top three constitutional offices—president, vice-president, and prime minister—were all occupied by RSS men? As we have seen, the RSS has long held the belief that the Constitution of India is fundamentally flawed. The RSS has, therefore, strongly taken the position that the Constitution must be rewritten to create their notion of a Hindu rashtra, an intention of which the novelist and activist Arundhati Roy has written: 'That idea turns everything that is beautiful about India into acid.'[11]

But interestingly, the RSS's current sarsanghchalak, Mohan Bhagwat, has apparently abandoned this long-held view. The Constitution, he declared in Delhi, is no longer such a flawed document. 'The RSS accepts the Constitution. There is not even one example in which the RSS has done anything against the Constitution,' Bhagwat declared. 'The Constitution is the consensus of our country. Following the Constitution is everyone's duty,' he added.[12] From anyone else, that would be a mere statement of the obvious; coming from Mohan Bhagwat, the head of the organization that has always espoused an alternative idea of India, it seems an earth-shaking affirmation. What about Hindu rashtra? Bhagwat did not disavow the term; he merely redefined it. 'Hindu rashtra,' he explained, 'does not mean it has no place for Muslims. The day it is said that Muslims are unwanted here, the concept of Hindutva will cease to exist.'[13]

---

[11] Arundhati Roy, 'India: Intimations of an Ending', *The Nation*, 22 November 2019.
[12] '"Muslims, Constitution, Hindutva...": How Mohan Bhagwat is Allaying Fears at RSS Meet', *News18*, 19 September 2018.
[13] Lalmani Verma, 'If Muslims are unwanted, then there is no Hindutva: Mohan Bhagwat at RSS event', *Indian Express*, 19 September 2018.

It is, of course, pertinent to ask whether we should take the Hindutvavadis' claims to be admirers of the present secular, liberal, Western-influenced Constitution of India to be as sincere as their professions of devotion to Upadhyaya. Will the votaries of Hindutva, having failed in the elections of 2024 to consolidate their hold on both the Lok Sabha and the Rajya Sabha, be willing to abandon their long-expressed desire to tear up the very Constitution to which they have now so enthusiastically pledged allegiance? A close reading of the works of its principal ideologues, notably Deen Dayal Upadhyaya, suggests that amending the Constitution was for long high on the ruling party's priority list.[14] Has that changed, and will they decide, as Mohan Bhagwat's words seem to suggest, that they do not need to, for after all as Ambedkar had warned, the Constitution itself could be perverted in its application to ensure that it protected a majoritarianism it did not envisage?

Whether or not the BJP goes full tilt at rewriting the entire Constitution to establish the Hindu rashtra of its dreams, or decides to create a majoritarian state politically without amending the Constitution, an obvious first step in that direction is probable. The easy target our ruling party could aim at is to reverse a key interpolation of the Forty-second Amendment of the Constitution, which in 1976 added two words the BJP doesn't like—'secular' and 'socialist'—to the Preamble. During the Constituent Assembly Debates, the economist K. T. Shah had tried and failed on 15 November 1948 to achieve inclusion of the words 'Secular, Federalist,

---

[14] See Shashi Tharoor, 'The cat is finally out of the bag: Hindutva leaders' utter disdain for the Indian Constitution', *The Print*, 26 December 2017.

Socialist' in the Preamble.[15] In the eventual compromise, the majority of the Assembly took the view that the Indian state would indeed be secular but that it was not necessary to use the word in the Preamble.

The issue with the theory of secularism in India is that it is officially translated as dharma-nirpekshata (keeping apart from dharma), which is impossible for any good Hindu to adhere to, rather than as panth-nirpekshata (not favouring any particular sect or faith). I have long argued that 'secularism' is a misnomer in the Indian context of profuse religiosity, and what we should be talking about is 'pluralism'. The roots of India's pluralism can be found in the Hindu philosophy of acceptance of difference: Ekam Sat viprah bahudha vadanti, the Truth is one but the wise call it by many names.

Pluralism has meant the active encouragement of religion in this country, in defiance of classical secular theory. Indian secularism embraces financial support to religious schools and the persistence of 'personal law' for different religious communities. The Hindutva brigade does not like this, and it is determined to do away with it. They argue that the practice of secularism has meant the uncritical acceptance of regressive practices among the Muslim community while demanding progressive behaviour from Hindus, support for minority education while denying such aid to Hindus, promotion of 'family planning' among Hindus but not enforcing it among Muslims, cultivation of 'vote banks' led by conservative Muslim leaders but the disparagement of their Hindu equivalents, and so on. At the same time, this

---

[15] Adrija Roychowdhury, 'Secularism: Why Nehru dropped and Indira inserted the S-word in the Constitution', *Indian Express,* 4 June 2020.

widespread denunciation of the 'appeasement' of Muslims is contradicted by statistical evidence of Muslim socio-economic backwardness and the prevalence of discrimination in such areas as housing and employment. Muslims are under-represented in the nation's police forces and over-represented in its prisons. Yet, Hindutva leaders have successfully stoked a perception that government benefits are skewed towards minorities, and thus justified their campaign for Hindu self-assertiveness.

It is for such reasons that Deen Dayal Upadhyaya had argued that secularism would have to go: in his words, it 'implies opposition of Hindus and appeasement of Muslims or other minorities. We should get rid of this word as soon as possible. It is completely irrelevant in the Indian context'.[16]

The word 'secularism', after all, was explicitly Western in origin, emerging from the political changes in Europe that accompanied the Protestant Reformation and the era called the Enlightenment. But many twentieth century leaders outside Western Europe were attracted to the concept, notably Kemal Atatürk in Muslim-majority Turkey, and Jawaharlal Nehru in Hindu-majority India, both of whom saw a secular state as a crucial hallmark of modernity. In India's case, secularism also seemed to Nehru the only way to avoid the religious and communal antagonisms that had partitioned the country when the British left.

The Constituent Assembly Debates show the extent to which this logic was accepted by our Founding Fathers. 'I accepted this secularism in the sense that our State shall

---

[16] Quoted in Shashi Tharoor, *Why I am a Hindu*, New Delhi: Aleph Book Company, 2018, p. 191.

remain unconcerned with religion, and I thought that the secular State of partitioned India was the maximum of generosity of a Hindu dominated territory for its non-Hindu population,' said Lokanath Misra in the debate on 6 December 1948.[17]

But was it necessary to include the word itself in the Constitution? The chairman of the Drafting Committee, Dr B. R. Ambedkar, thought not. He said: 'What should be the policy of the State, how the Society should be organised in its social and economic side are matters which must be decided by the people themselves according to time and circumstances. It cannot be laid down in the Constitution itself because that is destroying democracy altogether.'[18]

Still, the adoption of Articles 25, 26, 27, and 28 of the Constitution, guaranteeing freedom of conscience and the right to profess, practise, and propagate one's religion, to manage one's own religious affairs, and to enjoy the freedom of religious worship, confirmed that the concept of secularism was unarguably implicit in India's constitutional philosophy. But it wasn't Western-style secularism, which meant irreligiousness, which even avowedly atheist parties like the Communists or the various manifestations of the southern DMK movement found unpopular amongst their voters. Rather, secularism meant, in the Indian tradition, a profusion of religions, none of which was privileged by the state—which (in Amartya Sen's words) preserved an 'equidistance' from, and an 'equal symmetry' of treatment

---

[17] *Constituent Assembly of India Debates (Proceedings)*, Vol. VII, 6 December 1948.
[18] Jayita Mukhopadhyay, 'Ambedkar's vision of a secular Constitution', *The Statesman*, 6 April 2018.

of, all religions.[19] One can credibly argue that the Forty-second Amendment merely put a word into the Constitution whose spirit was always deeply embedded in it, and reified in governmental practice.

So can the word be taken out? The loss of the word 'secularism' will not necessarily make the country less secular, since successive Indian governments had practised the peculiar Indian variant of secularism anyway before the Forty-second Amendment. Nor can we convincingly protest a further amendment to a Constitution we have already amended more than a hundred times before.

But to remove the word 'secular' would be no ordinary amendment—even if that alone cannot change the secular nature of the Constitution, the signal it would send would be chilling. The BJP home minister, Amit Shah, says his government has no intention of removing the word 'secular' from the Preamble.[20] But should others in the party, in keeping with Upadhyaya's wishes, seek to do so, the nation must and will resist the BJP's attempts—not because the word itself is essential, but because its removal will symbolize an assault on the spirit of Indian pluralism and religious freedom. This spirit, it must be remembered, was not created by the Constitution but reflected in it.

Of course, such a change would first have to pass the test of judicial review against the yardstick of the Supreme Court's historic 1973 judgement in *Kesavananda Bharati Sripadagalvaru & Ors. vs State of Kerala, 1973*, outlining the 'Basic Structure' of the Constitution, which includes

---

[19] Sen, *The Argumentative Indian*.
[20] 'Amit Shah says there is no need to remove "secular" from Constitution', *India Today*, 19 April 2024.

secularism. If it survives that test, and if Indian liberals fail in preventing the removal of the word 'secularism', we must never stop fighting to preserve its spirit in the political practice of our country. But the task has been made easier by the Supreme Court's 2024 judgement rejecting writ petitions filed in 2020, forty-four years after the words 'socialist' and 'secular' became integral to the Preamble, seeking their deletion. These terms, the court opined, 'have achieved widespread acceptance, with their meanings understood by "We, the people of India" without any semblance of doubt. The additions to the Preamble have not restricted or impeded legislations or policies pursued by elected governments, provided such actions did not infringe upon fundamental and constitutional rights or the basic structure of the Constitution. Therefore, we do not find any legitimate cause or justification for challenging this constitutional amendment after nearly 44 years.' The Court declared that 'the constitutional position remains unambiguous'.[21]

The Supreme Court's recent decision would surely be a hurdle for any attempt aimed at removing the words 'secular' or 'socialist'. The judgement states, in context of this word—'In essence, the concept of secularism represents one of the facets of the right to equality, intricately woven into the basic fabric that depicts the constitutional scheme's pattern.'[22]

Aside from the word 'secular', majoritarian opinion is

---

[21] *Balram Singh vs Union of India on 9 February, 2024* (Writ Petition (Civil) No. 645/2020); Anmol Kaur Bawa, '"No Legitimate Cause": Supreme Court Dismisses Pleas Challenging Inclusion of Words "Socialist" & "Secular" In Constitution's Preamble', *Live Law*, 25 November 2024.
[22] Ibid.

also irritated by the prevalence of a practice like Muslim Personal Law, which—dealing as it does with matters of marriage, adoption, divorce, and inheritance—in no way impinges on the Hindu community. Despite this, the drafting of a uniform civil code (UCC) is also on the BJP agenda—once again as a way of putting Indian Muslims firmly in their place. While listed in Article 44 as a directive principle the state was to aspire to, a uniform civil code was long considered a desirable objective but one that could not be realized without the consent and cooperation of all communities—which was unlikely to be forthcoming, since most minority groups saw their own personal laws as entrenched in practice and 'acquired rights' in Indian law over several centuries.[23] Nehru had never opposed the idea of a uniform civil code in principle, but always argued that it required all communities to go along voluntarily. In 1954, he declared, 'I do not think that the time is right in India for me to try to push it through.' This remained the broad view of all governments until the BJP government formally proposed a rethink on the issue in 2024.

A UCC would replace personal laws based on religious scriptures and customs with a common set of laws governing every citizen. Proponents argue that a UCC would ensure equality before the law by providing the same legal framework for all citizens, regardless of religion, and promote national unity and integration by creating a common identity for all citizens. This would eliminate discriminatory practices in

---

[23] For example, Muslims are governed by the Muslim Personal Law (Shariat) Application Act, 1937, and the Dissolution of Muslim Marriages Act, 1939; Christians by the Indian Christian Marriage Act, 1872, and the Indian Divorce Act, 1869; and Zoroastrians by the Parsi Marriage and Divorce Act, 1936.

personal laws, particularly those affecting women. Having a single set of laws would also simplify the legal system, making it easier to administer justice and reduce the burden on the judiciary. Some also support a UCC on secular grounds, arguing that it would strengthen India's secular fabric by ensuring that laws are not influenced by religious doctrines. But many who hold this view also add that it cannot be imposed on the unwilling.

There is already a UCC in the state of Goa, a legacy of Portuguese colonialism. This legal framework, known as the Goa Civil Code or Goa Family Law, based on the Portuguese Civil Code of 1867 (which was retained even after Goa became a part of India in 1961), governs personal matters such as marriage, divorce, and succession for all residents of Goa. Hindus, Muslims, Christians, and others in the state are all governed by the same set of laws for personal matters. The code provides for monogamous marriages and outlines the procedures for divorce, including mutual consent and fault-based grounds; ensures equal inheritance rights for sons and daughters and provides for the division of property among heirs; and permits adoption, with adopted children enjoying the same legal rights as biological children. It is widely considered to have worked well—in particular, in promoting gender equality and streamlining legal processes—and there is no opposition to it within Goa. As a result, the implementation of the UCC in Goa has been largely successful and is often cited as a model for the rest of India. But Goa's history is very different from that of the rest of India.

Opponents of a national UCC argue that it would undermine India's cultural and religious diversity by imposing a uniform set of laws on all communities. They believe that personal laws are an integral part of religious and cultural identity. They are also concerned that a UCC could infringe on the rights of religious minorities, adding to the sense of alienation and marginalization many already feel. Nonetheless, the BJP government in the state of Uttarakhand passed a law in 2024 to implement a UCC in the state, which is overwhelmingly (83 per cent) Hindu in population, and began implementing it in January 2025.

Aside from imposing a uniform set of laws on all communities, regardless of their religious beliefs and practices, and thereby undermining India's cultural and religious diversity, the Uttarakhand UCC has reignited debates about the balance between individual rights, religious freedoms, and the constitutional vision of a secular and egalitarian society. The mandatory registration of live-in relationships required by the UCC has raised concerns about privacy and individual autonomy, and state intrusion into personal lives. While the Uttarakhand UCC claims to promote gender equality, provisions such as the mandatory registration of live-in relationships (and declaration of prior relationships) would not effectively safeguard women's rights and could potentially expose them to societal judgement and discrimination. The practical implementation of the UCC may face challenges, including resistance from various communities and the need for extensive administrative and legal infrastructure to enforce the new laws, including on Uttarakhand residents temporarily residing outside the state, in jurisdictions where older personal laws apply.

Whatever the outcome of the national debate—and it is by no means clear, as these words are written, that the ruling party has the votes, or the political capital, to get its way on this issue nationally—it is evident that implementing a UCC across India would be a complex and challenging task, given the vast diversity of customs and practices across different communities in India. It is not yet clear what specific provisions a national UCC would contain, and which current practices of which communities would be affected by its passage. A large number of suggestions from the public received by the Law Commission have yet to be processed. It remains to be seen which of these views will prevail. Interestingly, the 22nd Law Commission was finally wound up on 31 August 2024, without submitting a report on the Uniform Civil Code.

IX

A Union of States

The ultimate restraint on authoritarianism taking over India lies in its constitutional federalism, especially with many states ruled by other political parties, but the word 'federal' is nowhere to be found in the text of the Constitution, and the federal aspects of our quasi-federal state are blithely ignored by authoritarian central governments in their headlong rush to dominance. Addressing the concern that the Constitution is anti-federal and tilts the balance in favour of the union, Dr Ambedkar explained to the Constituent Assembly in 1949 that the 'Centre and the States are co-equal' in matters of legislative and executive authority. He added the clarification that the overriding powers given to the union in the Constitution are only 'to be used in an emergency'. In other words, he averred, the regular conduct of the business of democracy in India would take place within a federal framework and not a unitary one. The judiciary has played its part in reaffirming this credo and finding federalism in the basic structure of the Constitution, beginning with the judgement in *S. R. Bommai vs Union of India, 1994*, and continuing to the *Government of NCT of Delhi vs Union of India, 2024*.

Still, the Constitution gives the executive a much freer hand in practice than its lofty language about a 'Union of

States' suggests. Ambedkar was categorical that the federal nature of the Constitution was limited to the independence of the legislature and the executive of both the union and the states; as he pointed out, the federation had not emerged as a result of an agreement by the states to create a union, but the other way around. Ambedkar argued that the union was 'indestructible' and 'no state has the right to secede from it'.

The provision under Article 356, entitling the central government to declare President's Rule in a state, remained for many years the most powerful indication of the constitutional imbalance in favour of the union government vis-à-vis the states. Though, in introducing it in the draft Constitution, Ambedkar had described the provision as one that would be resorted to very rarely, and that would largely 'remain a dead letter', Article 356 was resorted to with alarming frequency by successive governments. Prime Minister Indira Gandhi alone invoked Article 356 no fewer than fifty times, and it has been imposed 125 times in the seventy-five-year history of the Constitution. In 1993, the Supreme Court, in *S. R. Bommai vs the Union of India*, decided that any future use of Article 356 would be subject to judicial review, a ruling that has had a significantly restrictive effect on its employment and further misuse.

The Emergency of 1975–77 and the national lockdown during the Covid-19 pandemic of 2020–21 are cases in point that demonstrate the dominance of the central or union government. Decentralization, deliberation, dissent, and debate—indeed the substance of democracy itself—were all treated as dispensable in times of crisis. They are seen as desirable rhetorical ideals best reserved for 'normal' times. During the Emergency, among significant political and civil rights abuses, thousands of political opponents, activists, and dissenters were arrested and detained without trial, the media was censored and fundamental rights, including the right to free speech, assembly, and press, were suspended. Opposition state governments were dismissed, judicial review curtailed, coercive sterilizations, and slum demolitions conducted and elections postponed. For the several months of the Covid-19 lockdown, Parliament remained non-functional, with committees refused authorization to meet virtually, and governmental accountability to the legislature, for all practical purposes, suspended. All of these acts were undemocratic, but arguably constitutional. Sometimes the 'crisis' is man-made, like the abrupt decision to demonetize 86 per cent of India's currency (by value) at a few hours' notice in November 2016, leading to catastrophic consequences for millions of families, businesses, and workers. Again, there was no viable challenge to the arbitrariness of the executive.

Though the Constitution envisages a federal structure with many powers reserved to the states, it gives the centre overriding authority over the states, both financially and administratively, as well as the power to redraw the national map by dividing states, creating new states, and converting states into union territories (and vice versa). The national government tells the states what they can do, and grants or withholds funds the states need to perform their functions. Nowhere was this more apparent than during the Emergency; it was also evident when the coronavirus pandemic began sweeping the world in 2020, and the Modi regime invoked a little-known provision of the National Disaster Management Act, 2005, to impose a nationwide lockdown (at just over three hours' notice) without even a pretence of consulting the elected chief ministers of governments in the states. Ironically, Entries 1 and 6 of the State List grant the states the legislative and executive powers over public order and public health. Further, Article 243W, read with the Twelfth Schedule (Entry 6), encourages states to delegate their responsibilities over public health to municipalities. The centre only has powers over preventing the spread of diseases from one state to another (under Entry 29 of the Concurrent List)[1]. Yet no judge ruled against this overreaching exercise of authority by the central government.

Many regional parties are acutely conscious of their dependence on the largesse of the central government and their vulnerability to the authority of New Delhi. Some have made a Faustian bargain with the government—do what you like at the national level as long as you leave us alone in our states. Even in those states where the BJP is not in power but regional parties are, they have proven all too willing to negotiate with the central government in order to navigate their way through its authoritarianism, rather than resist it. The result is a reconfiguration of India's federal diversity in the service of the nationalist project; the BJP's hyper-nationalism remains unchallenged even in the name of federalism.

The constitutional intent in India, articulated by successive governments over several decades, and particularly since the adoption of panchayati raj (village self-government) legislation in the early 1990s, was to promote greater decentralization of decision-making. Traditional self-governance through institutions of local governance had been supplanted by British colonial rule through the imposition of a 'collector' in

---

[1] See, in this regard, Kevin James, 'Covid-19 and the Need for Clear Centre-State Roles,' Vidhi Centre for Legal Policy, 3 April 2020.

every district, answerable not to the locals but to the imperial government. With this unitary inheritance, independent India sought, fitfully, to revert greater power and authority to institutions of local self-government (while still retaining the collector and the top-down administrative system around him). This process of increasing decentralization has come to a halt in recent years, while the intermediate layer of governance, the states, have found the balance tilting against them.

While Narendra Modi, prime minister when this book was written, has spoken piously of his faith in 'competitive-co-operative federalism[2]', this has turned out to be a mantra without a method. The centre has ridden roughshod over the states on all issues that matter, kept an ever-larger share of the nation's revenues for itself and starved states of resources, so that state governments can no longer easily pursue their own priorities.[3] A list summarizing the practice of centralism under Modi would include: the disastrous demonetization of the currency, with no warning to state governments;[4] the skewing of fiscal federalism towards the union from the states, which are bearing the brunt of the dual regime of Finance Commission allocations and an iniquitous Goods and Services Tax (GST), compounded by the imposition of a variety of 'cesses' over and above regular taxes, which would go entirely to the central government and not be part of the divisible pool of revenue shared with

---

[2] '"We need competitive-cooperative federalism": PM Modi on allegations of "insufficient support" to state govts', *Economic Times*, 16 April 2024.
[3] Samreen Wani, 'The Centre's share in States' revenue has surged in the last decade', *The Hindu*, 14 January 2025.
[4] Jammi N. Rao, 'Demonetisation at 6: The idea, the objectives, and the post-event justifications', *News Laundry*, 8 November 2022.

the states; efforts to foist Hindi upon the southern states[5]; the deployment of independent regulatory and investigative agencies (such as the ED, CBI, and Income Tax agencies) to clamp down on political opponents from regional parties[6]; the imposition of a nationwide lockdown without consulting the chief ministers who had to implement it[7]; the creation and opaque control of the 'PM Cares fund', which limited the flow of cash to state-run Chief Minister's Distress Relief Funds[8]; and the abrogation of Article 370 (and doing Jammu and Kashmir out of its statehood) in a manner that sets an ominous precedent for all other states.

The insertion of Article 370 into the Constitution, making special provision for Jammu and Kashmir, occurred at the request of the Kashmiri nationalist leader, Sheikh Abdullah, which was endorsed by Prime Minister Nehru over the objections of Ambedkar and Sardar Patel. Nehru entrusted its drafting to Gopalaswami Ayyangar, who had served in Kashmir and liaised closely with Sheikh Abdullah in crafting its provisions.[9] There were several objections to

---

[5] Hannah Ellis-Petersen, '"A threat to unity": anger over push to make Hindi national language of India', *The Guardian*, 25 December 2022.

[6] '"Politicians Can't Claim Higher Immunity": Supreme Court Refuses To Entertain Plea Of 14 Opposition Parties Against 'Misuse' Of CBI & ED, *Live Law*, 5 April 2023; Deeptiman Tiwary, 'Since 2014, 4-fold jump in ED cases against politicians; 95% are from Opposition', *Indian Express*, 21 September 2022; Deeptiman Tiwary, 'Since 2014, 25 Opposition leaders facing corruption probe crossed over to BJP, 23 of them got reprieve', *Indian Express*, 4 April 2024.

[7] Sobhana K. Nair, 'Coronavirus: PM should have consulted State govts. before announcing lockdown, says Chhattisgarh CM Bhupesh Baghel', *The Hindu*, 21 March 2020.

[8] 'PM CARES: How the Union govt projects ownership but evades transparency', *News Minute*, 10 February 2023.

[9] Seema Chishti, 'Sheikh Abdullah, Ayyangar, Sardar Patel: How Article 370 was negotiated, debated', *Indian Express*, 6 August 2019; Makkhan

it within the Congress Working Committee, as well as in the Constituent Assembly, all contesting the need for any one state to enjoy specific constitutional provisions denied to other states, but it finally was included in the constitution under the heading 'Temporary, Transitional and Special provisions'.[10] Its abrogation by an Act of Parliament in 2019 proved controversial because of the manner in which it occurred—with the state's elected legislative assembly suspended, President's Rule in operation, and the assent of the appointed governor serving as the consent of the state—but in the several years since, appears to have found broad acceptance, with few non-Kashmiri political parties calling for its restoration.[11]

In 2023, Tamil Nadu Chief Minister M. K. Stalin sent a letter to the chief ministers of non-BJP-ruled states on the subject of federalism, appealing to them to join him in resisting the encroachments of the union government. 'The Constitution of India has clearly defined the roles and responsibilities of the Union and State Governments along with the role of the Governor. However, it is observed that such time-tested principles are neither respected nor followed now, affecting the functioning of state governments.'[12] The governor's delay in clearing bills brought 'state administrations to a standstill', he added, urging that there should be 'a time limit for Governors to

---

Lal, 'Kashmir, Nehru's Idealism and Article 370', VifIndia.org, 4 July 2018.
[10] 'Article 370 of Indian Constitution in Hindi', Constitution of India.
[11] 'Article 370: What happened with Kashmir and why it matters', *BBC*, 6 August 2019; Meryl Sebastian and Sharanya Hrishikesh, 'Article 370: India Supreme Court upholds repeal of Kashmir's special status', *BBC*, 11 December 2023.
[12] Arun Janardhanan, 'Governors stalling Bills: Stalin writes to non-BJP ruled states seeking common stand', *Indian Express*, 13 April 2023.

approve the bills passed by the respective legislatures'[13]. The role of the union-appointed governor has become a source of contention in many Opposition-ruled states, with accusations of political bias allegedly colouring some gubernatorial actions. This was certainly not the intention of the framers of the Constitution.

There is an even more significant problem looming. In 1976, the omnibus Forty-second Amendment to the Constitution decided to freeze the allocation of Lok Sabha seats for twenty-five years to encourage population control, by assuring states that success in limiting population would not lose them Lok Sabha seats. In 2001, the NDA government of Prime Minister Vajpayee extended this arrangement for another twenty-five years; its proposal, which became the Eighty-fourth Amendment, was unanimously adopted by all parties in both houses of Parliament.

The thinking behind this policy was clear: it was based on the sound principle that the reward for responsible stewardship by a state of demography and human development could not be political disenfranchisement. While there is some logic to the argument that a democracy must value all its citizens equally—whether they live in a progressive state or one that, by failing to empower its women and reducing total fertility, has allowed its population to shoot through the roof—no federal democracy can survive the perception that states would lose political clout if they develop well, while others would gain more seats in Parliament as a reward for failure.

Is the Modi government delaying the 2021 census—

Shilpa Nair, 'Tamil Nadu CM MK Stalin writes to non-BJP states over ernors "indefinitely" holding bills', *India Today*, 12 April 2023.

initially kept in abeyance because of Covid, and now unconscionably delayed—in order to conduct it so that its results are announced after the Eighty-fourth Amendment lapses in 2026? This would confirm what many in the South fear—that the burgeoning population of the northern Hindi-speaking 'cow belt' states would lead to a dramatic expansion in their seats in the Lok Sabha, at the expense of the population-controlling southern states. Already there is a growing consciousness of a North–South divide in financial matters: while Karnataka meets 72 per cent[14] of its expenses from the state's own taxes, Bihar gets about 75 per cent[15] of its expenses from central taxes. On 10 January 2025, Uttar Pradesh received a whopping ₹31,039 crores of tax devolution,[16] a figure greater than all the five southern states collectively received. In other words, unlike most federal systems, India's revenues are going disproportionately to its worst-performing states, those with poor levels of education, high rates of fertility and population growth, while the high-performance states in the south get short shrift. If political clout is lost as well, the entire constitutional edifice could come under strain.

The government's answer would be that those are the rules of democracy—one-person-one-vote means the more people you have, the more political clout, and tax rupees,

---

[14] 'Finances of the State Government', Report on State Finances for the year ended 31 March 2013, p. 12.
[15] 'Evaluation of State Finances in Bihar', Patna: Asian Development Research Institute, 2018, p. ix.
[16] Ministry of Finance, 'Union Government releases tax devolution of ₹1,73,030 crore to State Governments to accelerate capital spending and finance their development and welfare-related expenditures', PIB Delhi, 10 January 2025; 'Kerala receives Rs 3,330.83 crore as Centre releases tax devolution to state governments', *Mathrubhumi*, 10 January 2025.

you get. But in a country like India, whose diversity is held together by a sense of common belonging but whose civic nationalism must accommodate a range of states with divergent levels of development, it is essential that all feel that their common nationhood is a winning proposition for them. In a country where regional, religious, and linguistic tensions are never far from the surface, such an answer—'we have more people, so we will have more money and more power'—risks rupturing the bonds that hold us all together. The concerns of the southern states about delimitation are not unfounded: Uttar Pradesh and Bihar are likely to together have the seats in Parliament to outweigh them all combined. The interests of millions are entwined with the need for an effective compromise, in which the principles of equitable redistribution and representation should weigh heavily. All states, ultimately, must work together to devise a solution.

India is united not by a common ethnicity, language, or religion, but by the experience of a common history within a shared geographical space, reified in a liberal Constitution, and the repeated exercise of democratic self-governance in a pluralist polity. India's Founding Fathers wrote a Constitution for this dream; we in India have given passports to their ideals. The India of tomorrow will only flourish if it resists the undermining of its strengths by a rampant Hindu nationalism, strengthens its civic institutions, and shores up its liberal democracy. It is time to reaffirm the patriotic idea of India enshrined in our Constitution—to separate the powers and roles of the legislature, the judiciary, and the executive, to ensure that the first two do not become mere rubber stamps for the third, and to reaffirm the powers of the states, so that no government can unilaterally abrogate the rights of any Indian. 'India's Constitution,' wrote Rajendra Prasad, the first president of India, 'is a testament to the power of inclusive governance and the rule of law.' It needs to be that again. That is the challenge that awaits India in the twenty-first century.

Conclusion

Our liberal, inclusive, and just Constitution, based unambiguously on the principles of civic nationalism, has been the bedrock of our society, a guiding document that historically secured the inalienable rights of all Indians. It has not only consolidated and distilled the best of our democratic values, ideas for which our forefathers gave their lives at the height of our nationalist struggle, but has served to liberate the collective aspirations of our people. In the remarkable work of the Constituent Assembly, the Constitution served as a reminder that our country was always greater than the sum of our differences and that our diversity of thought, expression, and ideology was, and can be, our greatest strength. The Constitution allowed each Indian to create their individual political identity and thus collectively to fashion the nation's destiny. But, as Ambedkar warned, a Constitution is only as good as those who work it. That is where, sadly, India seems today to be falling short.

Over the past decade, the Constitution and the values it embodies—especially those of liberty, equality, and fraternity, all woven together by secular pluralism—have been threatened. Its most seminal contribution to the idea of India, that of the primacy of liberty and autonomy, and of the individual citizen being the true custodian of her republic, has been brutalized. Dissent in particular has been villainized as anti-national, with dissidents charged under draconian antiterrorism laws, notably the Unlawful Activities (Prevention) Act (UAPA), which turn the process into the punishment. This ensures that an undertrial languishes endlessly in prison before—as has occurred in 97 per cent of the cases filed under UAPA[1]—being acquitted for lack of evidence. Today our Constitution's pluralist, progressive, and peaceful idea of India faces numerous perils, as do the institutions and watchdogs entrusted with safeguarding it and fending off authoritarian impulses and brute majoritarianism. As for the repressive sedition law, which has not even spared university students shouting slogans over the previous decade in India—all thanks to the loose, colonially motivated wording of the law—the government claims to have jettisoned it by rehauling the Indian Penal Code. Yet, as even a cursory glance at Section 152 of this new, ostensibly decolonized Bharatiya Nyaya Sanhita 2023, makes evident, sedition has merely been split into a series of vaguely defined, stringently punishable offences. The spectre of an authoritarian, vindictive, surveillance state thus continues looming large over India.

In 2024, we celebrated the seventy-fifth anniversary of the adoption of our Constitution with great pomp and pageantry. But the self-congratulatory rhetoric could not paper over the glaring cracks that have appeared in the fortifications of our constitutional structure and grow wider by the day, rendering the principles of the Constitution vulnerable to alarming onslaughts. The increasing centralization of power within the executive of the union government, already enabled by the quasi-federal structure of the Constitution, has been exacerbated by governmental practice in riding roughshod over

---

[1] Rajulapudi Srinivas, 'UAPA should be scrapped as 97 percent accused are aquitted, says Prof. Haragopal', *The Hindu*, 28 January 2024.

the states. It has become impossible to escape the perception that increasingly, our elections sustain only the bare bones of democracy, even as its sinews—our Parliament, legislatures, judiciary, news media, civil society, public universities, and watchdog agencies—are either hollowed out or hijacked. Parliament, whose capacity to demand accountability of the executive has been compromised by the Tenth Schedule in 1985 (the 'anti-defection law') enforcing the authority of the party over its MPs, has been further weakened in recent years by the brute majority enjoyed by the ruling party. Fundamental rights have been abridged by governments with impunity under constitutional clauses permitting wide leeway to state governments, including clauses allowing for administrative detention. More pernicious still is the current politics of religious hatred, vigilantism in the name of religion, the demonizing of minorities, and the brazen communalization of our politics, polity, and public life.

Over the past decade, concerted efforts have been made to reduce our Parliament from a vigorous forum of deliberation and dialogue to a noticeboard and rubber stamp for the ruling party's agenda.[2] The Supreme Court has seemed to slacken as well, losing the progressive zeal that animated the judgements recognizing the Right to Privacy and decriminalizing homosexuality; it has done little to hold an overweening executive to account and protect personal liberties, let alone advance them. Add to this the weaponization of investigative agencies (such as the ED, CBI, and Income Tax Department) against political opponents and

---

[2] Maansi Verma, 'Agenda Control in the Indian Parliament and the Impact on its Oversight Function – Analysis and Evidence', *Socio-Legal Review*, Volume 18, Issue 1, 2022.

dissidents, and the battering into submission of the Election Commission[3], the hollowing out of many of the institutions created by the Constitution (whose autonomy in any case was hampered by the powers of appointment remaining with the executive, which retains a majority in the selection committee for those appointments subject to consultation), and the constant undermining of the democratic spirit, India's democracy is under extraordinary strain. Indeed, the V-Dem Institute has already labelled India as an 'electoral autocracy'[4]. Such an autocracy, policed by the 'constable' Ambedkar warned against, survives on a crippling environment of fear that undermines the rule of the Constitution. Many today speak of an 'undeclared Emergency'. Taken together, these trends represent our Constitution-makers' worst fears—as Ambedkar had warned, '[if] those who are called to work it, happen to be a bad lot'—and challenge the constitutional cornerstone of our democratic republic.

Dr Ambedkar, of course, had a solution for the problem that he anticipated three quarters of a century ago. He urged Indians to respect the principles of the Constitution, to resist

---

[3] '"Politicians Can't Claim Higher Immunity" : Supreme Court Refuses To Entertain Plea Of 14 Opposition Parties Against "Misuse" Of CBI & ED', *Live Law*, 5 April 2023; 'Opposition in Rajya Sabha alleges CBI, ED being used for political purposes', *Times of India*, 10 April 2017; Snigdhendu Bhattacharya, 'Will India's Election Commission Provide All Parties a Level Playing Field?', *The Diplomat*, 21 March 2024.
The Chief Election Commissioner is currently selected by a committee consisting of the Prime Minister, another Minister and the Leader of the Opposition, which grants the executive a two-thirds majority, though in 2023, the Supreme Court had decreed that a member of the judiciary should serve on the Committee until Parliament enacted a law (which went on to substitute the Chief Justice of India with a Union Minister). The entire process is under the review of the Supreme Court as this book goes to press.
[4] 'India "one of the worst autocratisers": V-Dem report on democracy', *The Hindu*, 11 March 2024.

one-man rule, to stand against attempts to divide the nation along lines of religion or caste. His timeless wisdom must guide us as we contemplate the reality of what is being done to our democracy in the onrush of events. Yet his very assumptions are contested ground today.

The Constitution, to risk a cliché, has stood the test of time, even if it has had to undergo repeated surgery in the process—106 amendments constituting some sort of global record. The adaptability of the Constitution to the ever-changing realities of national life has effectively made it a vehicle of social change. It has the exemplary in-built ability to adjust to the needs of the times through a democratic and representative process. In this it has fulfilled the three purposes Granville Austin identified in one of the earliest seminal studies of the Indian Constitution—to build a strong state, to promote democracy, and to facilitate a social revolution. Is it not time, then, to review its workings, to question its increasing centralization, to devolve greater powers to the states, to create new provisions to strengthen governmental accountability and to consider amendments to restrain the concentration of executive power?

Courts have crafted remedies to various problems in which the state was deemed to be acting inefficiently or insufficiently, from human rights to environmental practices. 'Public interest litigation' is an extraordinary development, under which individuals with no locus standi on an issue can petition the court to take cognizance of, and issue orders on, matters of public policy. But these are often arguably the domain of the legislature and the executive, and PILs raise uncomfortable questions of judicial encroachment on the powers and responsibilities of the other two branches of government. The Supreme Court has also evolved the concept of the 'basic structure' of the Constitution which cannot be altered even by constitutional amendment, a far-reaching doctrine whose full implications we are yet to discover. But this too has given rise to issues of judicial overreach and the authority of Parliament, which have not yet been resolved. India's judiciary is self-perpetuating, having so far retained exclusively to itself the right to make judicial appointments (which the government sought unsuccessfully to regulate through its National Judicial Appointments Commission Act, 2014, and Constitution (Ninety-ninth Amendment) Act, 2014). In India's democracy, there is an efficient, well-tried, and constitutional law-making system in place. It is hardly perfect, but then we can recall the famous remark attributed to the nineteenth-century German Chancellor Otto Von Bismarck, 'If you like laws and sausages, you should never watch either one being made.'

There is, of course, no substitute for an independent professional judiciary to keep a watch over this constitutional process, to ensure that Parliament is not swept away by an imperious executive with a landslide majority—the prescient warning that Ambedkar issued to the nation in 1949. Checks and balances can be frustrating for the impatient, and I have argued elsewhere that a directly elected executive—along the lines of the US, France, Brazil, or Sri Lanka—would be far more effective in achieving results in our fractious polity. But we have to make a success of the Constitution we have. Here a balance between the legislature and the judiciary is necessary, though it will always be a matter of dispute how far it is reasonable for the judiciary to go in its activism before we can legitimately accuse it of overreach. Yet there are areas in which the judiciary could arguably have been more proactive and robust in curbing the excesses of the executive; several chief justices have been accused of being too conciliatory towards the executive on matters deemed to be of importance to the government, including by delaying consideration of sensitive cases, deferring them to a time when any judgement would have been otiose, or not taking some matters up at all. Different courts, in different eras, have been characterized as fearless and original in their interpretations, and others as all too obliging in deferring to the wishes of the executive. Any simple conclusion about the role of the judiciary is therefore impossible.

Equally, the question of whether further changes would make the Constitution even better suited to the needs of a diverse multi-ethnic, multi-lingual, and multi-religious country like India, must be faced sooner rather than later. Our Constitution has been written for a plural society. It has protected and defended that pluralism by enshrining and expanding the rights of various minority groups, notably religious minorities, Dalits and women (but not yet fully those of the LGBTQ+ community). It is true that the tension between the Constitution's upholding of individual rights and liberties coexists uneasily with its framework of defence of communitarian and group rights. Yet constitutionalism has become the principal means of embodying justice to Dalits and the Constitution remains their own preferred tool to undo injustice. But recent events have proved that it can still be subverted, if not in principle then certainly in practice, by those who disrespect its pluralist convictions.

For decades the Constitution has worked to promote our people's progress through debate and consultation, respect for the Opposition and minority points of view, and deference to legal process. Such constraints are unfortunately being increasingly disrespected today—and not only by the ruling party's desire to promote a narrow-minded and sectarian nationalism that brooks no dissent, and which for the first time has made some Indians feel unsafe to be themselves in India. Even while paying lip service to the Constitution, the powers-that-be have undermined constitutional principles through the promotion of a divisive ideology that excludes minorities from its ambit. The propagators of Hindutva have injected a toxin into the veins of Indian society, straightjacketing the nation into an 'us vs them' paradigm that sidelines constitutional ideals like equality, secularism, and justice.[5] The hysteria over 'love jihad'[6] (the allegation that Muslim men are marrying women of other faiths to convert them to Islam) and the passage by several states of anti-conversion laws might well not pass the test of constitutionality in the face of Articles 25 and 26. The idea that an individual's freedom of religion (and the right to propagate one's faith to a prospective spouse) are dispensable in the face of imagined threats to a majoritarian religious identity ignores both the constitutional protections for the former and the absence of any provision for the latter.

Even as they are caught up in this exclusionary discourse, not enough Indians are engaging with the details of their constitutional provisions and rights. For its part, the judiciary has issued interesting judgements: in *Rev. Stanislaus vs State of Madhya Pradesh, 1977*, the Supreme Court upheld the constitutionality of anti-conversion laws in Madhya Pradesh and Odisha, stating that the right to propagate religion does not include the right to convert another person to

---

[5] 'BJP amplifies "ek hain toh safe hain" slogan with newspaper ad in Maharashtra', *India Today*, 11 November 2024.
[6] 'Factsheet: Love Jihad Conspiracy Theory', *Bridge*, 13 May 2024.

one's own religion. In contrast, in *Lata Singh vs State of Uttar Pradesh, 2006,* (though the specific case dealt with an inter-caste marriage) its decision upheld the protection of inter-religious marriages by the administration and police, indirectly allowing for the possibility of conversion as a consequence of such unions. Further, the Supreme Court has also recognized the right to change one's religion as a fundamental aspect of religious freedom. In *Shafin Jahan vs Asokan K. M., 2018,* the Court affirmed that adults have the right to choose their religion and marry according to their choice, emphasizing the importance of individual autonomy in matters of faith. Meanwhile, hostility to conversion gains ground across northern India.[7]

'Independence,' Ambedkar said in concluding his memorable speech to the Constituent Assembly in 1949, 'is no doubt a matter of joy. But let us not forget that this independence has thrown on us great responsibilities. By independence, we have lost the excuse of blaming the British for anything going wrong. If hereafter things go wrong, we will have nobody to blame except ourselves.' Today, let us vow to reduce the number of things we need to blame ourselves for—and let the Constitution show us the way.

The struggle continues. There is much to be done to make the Indian Constitution a potent force in the twenty-first century. Citizens still need to be educated about their constitutional rights and duties. Awareness campaigns and educational programmes can help succeeding generations understand the importance of the Constitution and the role it plays in their lives. Citizens should actively participate in

---

[7] M. P. Nathanael, 'In the shadow of the anti-conversion law', *Deccan Herald*, 25 December 2023.

democratic processes, such as voting, public consultations, and civic activities, to ensure that their voices are heard and their rights are protected. Courts can play a proactive role in interpreting and expanding constitutional provisions to address contemporary issues and protect fundamental rights against the encroachments of the executive. The judiciary should continue to uphold the values enshrined in the Constitution, ensuring justice, equality, and the rule of law. Legislatures—Parliament and the state assemblies—should enact laws that reflect the evolving needs of society while adhering to constitutional principles. This includes addressing issues like gender equality, environmental protection, and digital rights. They should also ensure transparency and accountability in their actions, promoting good governance and public trust. The same applies to the autonomous institutions like the Election Commission, Comptroller and Auditor General, and National Human Rights Commission, in which there has been an erosion of public trust; they should be strengthened to function independently and effectively. Institutions should work together to implement constitutional provisions and address the challenges that have arisen and been enumerated in this book. This includes more effective coordination and cooperation between central and state governments, as well as between different branches of government. By taking these steps, various sections of the country can ensure that the Indian Constitution remains a powerful and relevant document in the twenty-first century, guiding the nation towards progress and justice.

The Constitution has undoubtedly been indispensable in fulfilling the hopes and promises of the struggle for freedom. It has furnished the template and provided the platform to protect the citizen from both the arbitrary misuse of political power as well as the caprices of a divided society. In the process, the Constitution has both created and helped shape Indian nationhood. It has won the faith of the people, who have repeatedly reaffirmed their trust in its tenets. Despite all the stresses and strains that have beset it, the Constitution has held the Indian republic together and helped it meet the challenges of its democratic evolution.

There is no reason to lose hope. Over the past five years, democracy- and liberty-loving citizens of India have risen to reclaim our republic. Rescuing the Constitution of India from the highbrow preserves of courtrooms, legal chambers, and law schools, they have mobilized it and sent it into battle. In the biting cold of December 2019 and early 2020, lakhs of Indians across the country—from youngsters and students to the old, yet indomitable, women of Shaheen Bagh—poured into the streets in protest against the appalling Citizenship Amendment Act and National Register of Citizens, which gave legal colour to the two-nation theory. On those freezing nights wrapped in fog, countless Indians of all faiths and castes, speaking numerous languages, held aloft portraits of Ambedkar, Gandhi, and Nehru and chanted the Preamble in unison—as *one* people. As the electrifying cry of 'We, the People of India....' ripped through the darkness, the idea of India roared back to life, revitalizing our republic and promising to awaken us into that 'Heaven of Freedom' Tagore wrote so inspiringly about.

The Constitution will prevail as long as its spirit survives in the ordinary citizens of India.

Acknowledgements

Even a short book like this would not have seen the light of day without many helping hands. Thanks are due, first of all, to my friend and publisher David Davidar, who conceived the idea for this book, determined its subject and its length, and guided me skilfully through multiple drafts.

Thanks, next, to my young friend Katherine Abraham, who volunteered to help with the research, found a prodigious amount of relevant material and went above the call of friendship in checking and completing all the references and citations in the notes to the book. Thanks, too, to Sheeba Thattil and Baawa Sayan Bajaj, whose work on other projects turned out to be helpful in this one too; to Shounak Banerjee, my chief of staff and a lawyer himself, and to Shashank Shekhar, my legislative assistant, for thoughtful suggestions on the final draft.

Aienla Ozukum of Aleph did a masterful job of copy-editing the raw manuscript to a sheen; her professional competence and very pleasant efficiency have made her a joy to work with on several of my books.

A subject as important and contentious as the working of the Constitution of India deserves the application of many minds, many pens and many points of view. Several others, with far greater legal and scholarly credentials than I have, have attempted this task. Mine is a thinking citizen's modest contribution to reviewing our experience, analysing our practice and developing an understanding of how our Constitution has worked for the people of the world's largest democracy. It does not seek to be a comprehensive or authoritative account of the Constitution, but rather an introductory commentary that might whet the readers' appetite for deeper study of this remarkable document and its significance for the lives of all Indians. If it stimulates your interest, dear reader, it will have served its purpose.

Further Reading

Aribam, Angellica and Satyawali, Akash, *The Fifteen: The Lives and Times of the Women in India's Constituent Assembly*, New Delhi: Hachette India, 2024.

Austin, Granville, *The Indian Constitution: Cornerstone of a Nation*, New Delhi: Oxford University Press, 1999.

Bakshi, P. M., *Constitution of India*, New Delhi: Universal Law Publishing Company Limited, 2010.

Basu, Durga Das, *Introduction to the Constitution of India*, Calcutta: S. C. Sarkar, 1966.

Bharathi, K. S., *The Political Thought of Pandit Deendayal Upadhyaya*, New Delhi: Concept Publishing Company, 1988.

Bhargava, Rajeev (ed.), *Politics and Ethics of the Indian Constitution*, New Delhi: Oxford University Press, 2008.

Bhatia, Gautam, *The Transformative Constitution: A Radical Biography in Nine Acts*, New Delhi: HarperCollins Publishers, 2019.

———, *The Indian Constitution: Conversations with Power*, New Delhi: HarperCollins Publishers, 2025.

Bhishikar, C. P., *The Indian Constitution: Conversations with Power, Pt. Deendayal Upadhyay Ideology & Preception - Part - 5: Concept of The Rashtra*, New Delhi: Suruchi Prakashan, 2014.

De, Rohit, *A People's Constitution: The Everyday Life of Law in the Indian Republic*, Princeton & Oxford: Princeton University Press, 2018.

Dworkin, Ronald, *Freedom's Law: The Moral Reading of the American Constitution*, Cambridge: Harvard University Press, 1997.

Golwalkar, M. S., *Bunch of Thoughts*, New Delhi: Vikram Prakashan, 1966.

——*We, or Our Nationhood Defined*, Nagpur: Bharat Publications, 1939.

Habib, S. Irfan (ed.), *Indian Nationalism: The Essential Writings*, New Delhi: Aleph Book Company, 2017.

Kashyap, Subhash C., *Our Constitution: An Introduction to India's Constitution and Constitutional Law*, New Delhi: National Book Trust, India, 1994.

Khosla, Madhav, *India's Founding Moment: The Constitution of a Most Surprising Democracy*, Cambridge: Harvard University Press, 2020.

Madhav, Ram, *Our Constitution Our Pride*, New Delhi: Prabhat Prakashan, 2025.

Metcalf, Thomas R., *Forging the Raj: Essays on British India in the Heyday of Empire*, London: Oxford University Press, 2005.

Nariman S. Fali, *You Must Know Your Constitution*, New Delhi: Hay House Publishers, 2023.

Nehru, Jawaharlal, *Words of Freedom: Ideas of a Nation*, New Delhi: Penguin Books, 2010.

Patel, Vallabhbhai, *The Collected Works of Sardar Vallabhbhai Patel*, Vol. I, New Delhi: Konark Publishers, 1990.

Rousseau, Jean-Jacques, *The Social Contract and Discourses*, London: J. M. Dent & Sons, 1920.

Savarkar, V. D., *Essentials of Hindutva*, Mumbai: V. V. Kelkar, 1923.

Sen, Amartya, *The Argumentative Indian: Writings on Indian History, Culture, and Identity*, New York: Farrar, Straus and Giroux, 2005.

Shiva Rao, B., Menon, V. K. N., Kashyap, Subhash C., and Iyengar, N. K. N., *The Framing of India's Constitution*, New Delhi: Indian Institute of Public Administration, 1966.

Sinculus, Diodorus, *Diodorus of Sicily*, C. H. Oldfather (tr.), London: Heinemann, 1933.

Singh, Tripurdaman, *Sixteen Stormy Days: The Story of the First Amendment to the Constitution of India*, London: Bloomsbury Academic, 2024.

Tharoor, Shashi, *Ambedkar: A Life*, New Delhi: Aleph Book Company, 2022.

—— *India: From Midnight to the Millennium and Beyond*, London: Arcade Publishing, 1997.

—— *The Battle of Belonging: On Nationalism, Patriotism, and What It Means to Be Indian*, New Delhi: Aleph Book Company, 2020.

—— *Why I Am a Hindu*, New Delhi: Aleph Book Company, 2018.

Upadhyaya, Deendayal, *Rashtra Jeevan ki Disha*, Ramshankar Agnihotri, Bhanupratap Shukl (eds.), Lucknow: Lokhit Prakashan, 2010.